Anonymous

Archaic Rock Inscriptions

An account of the cup and ring markings on the sculptured stones of the old and

new worlds

Anonymous

Archaic Rock Inscriptions
An account of the cup and ring markings on the sculptured stones of the old and new worlds

ISBN/EAN: 9783743407312

Manufactured in Europe, USA, Canada, Australia, Japa

Cover: Foto ©Thomas Meinert / pixelio.de

Manufactured and distributed by brebook publishing software
(www.brebook.com)

Anonymous

Archaic Rock Inscriptions

ARCHAIC

Rock Inscriptions;

An Account of the

CUP & RING MARKINGS

ON THE

Sculptured Stones

OF THE

OLD AND NEW WORLDS.

A. READER, Orange Street, Red Lion Square, London.

1891.

PREFACE.

FROM the title of the present volume, it might be thought that the subject of which it treats is not germane to that of Nature Worship. A careful perusal of its contents will, we think, serve to dispel any such consideration, and evoke the conclusion that it forms a valuable and fitting companion to those of the series already published. All the information that could be obtained, either by research or personal observation has been collected into this work, which cannot fail to prove equally as interesting as its predecessors. The original purpose of these Rock Cuttings still remains a matter of conjecture, but we have some confidence that in the following pages will be found the key to a problem that has severely taxed the ingenuity of the Archæologist.

With these prefatory remarks, we commend our readers to the study of a new discovery of Primæval Archaic Workmanship, remarkable for its duplication in widely separated countries of the habitable globe.

CONTENTS.

CHAPTER VIII.

CHAPTER IX.

CHAPTER X.

ARCHAIC ROCK MARKINGS.

CHAPTER I.

Introductory—Varieties of Markings.

THE subject we are now approaching the consideration of, is comparatively a new one, with which perhaps few men are acquainted, and upon which at present but a limited amount of literature has been produced. It is only within the last half-century—or little more—that public attention has been attracted to it, and as yet very little has been done towards its elucidation. Indeed the whole matter has come up rather by accident than otherwise—the unintentional disturbance of a layer of turf which had been accumulating for centuries over the surface of a rock, having brought to view mysterious markings which excited the curiosity of the discoverers, and led to further search, and comparison of notes in different parts of the world. Quite in the early part of the present century, a Mr. J. C. Langlands noticed some curious figures, very much worn and defaced, upon a sandstone block near the great camp on Old Bewick Hill, in the county of Northumberland. Mr. Tate, Secretary of the Anthropological Society, etc., who has rendered excellent service in describing the sculptured rocks of the north of England, says that though strange and old world looking, these figures then presented an isolated fact, and he (Mr. Langlands) hesitated to connect them with by-past ages ; for they might have been the work of an ingenious shepherd, while resting on the hill ; but on finding some years afterwards, another incised stone of a similar character, on the same hill, he then formed the opinion that these sculptures were very ancient, and probably the work of the same people who erected the strong and complicated fort cresting the hill. To him belongs the honour of the first discovery of these archaic sculptures.

Time passed on, and then further discoveries were made by the Rev. Mr. Greenwell and others, which lent additional importance to what Mr. Langlands had found, and stimulated further research.

The astounding fact then became evident that in all parts of the world there existed ancient cuttings in the rocks so wonderfully similar, that it was easy to see that whatever was the signification in one case, was the signification in another. We shall conduct our readers to these different localities, and describe engraved rocks as they occur in each, after which we shall as far as our limits will allow, discuss the question as to their authorship and meaning.

The earliest notice of cup and ring marks inscribed upon British or other rocks, is that in Camden's Britannia, Gough's edition, vol. 3, London, 1789. Opposite page 603 is an engraving of one of these sculptured stones, and the reference to it on page 645 says :—" It represents a Druidical altar, discovered lying on the ground near the Rev. Mr. Hart's at Lynsfort, on Inis Oen, 1773. The greatest length is 28 ft., in breadth, 25 feet. It is full of rock basons, and in one corner is what is described as ' a block on which the human victims were slain, and never seen on an altar before'."

The best authorities who have duly weighed and discussed the rock cuttings in various parts of the world, have supplied us with seven distinct forms or types of cup and ring markings. First we have single cups. These are no more than shallow depressions in the surface of the rock, varying from an inch to three inches or more in diameter. Their depth is frequently no·more than half an inch, and seldom goes beyond an inch, still more rarely do they exceed an inch and a half, and they are found of these different sizes on the surface of the same rock or stone. They are generally found mixed up with ring cuttings. "Among the sculptured rock surfaces, for instance," says Sir John Simpson, "in Argyleshire, there are in one group at Auchnabreach, thirty-nine or forty cup-cuttings, and the same number of ring-cuttings ; and at Carnban there are twenty-nine figures,—namely nine single cups, seven cups surrounded by single rings, and thirteen cups encircled by a series of concentric rings."

"The simple cup-cuttings," proceeds Sir James, " are generally scattered singly, and apparently quite irregularly over the surface of the stone ; but occasionally they seem placed in groups of four, six, or more,—almost in a methodic and constellation-like arrangement. Usually the edge of the cup is smooth and regular in its circumference ; but occasionally it is depressed or guttered at one point, or on one side."

A second type of these markings consists of cups surrounded with a single ring or circle. According to the above authority the ring is usually very much shallower than the cup, and forms a sort of border or setting to it. The ring is often complete as a circle, but at other times it has a groove which sometimes extends from the central cup outwards beyond the ring. Occasionally the groove is in the edge only of the cup.

A third class consists of cups surrounded with a series of concentric complete rings, varying in number from two to six or seven, or more.

The fourth class consists of cups surrounded with a series of concentric but incomplete rings and having a straight radial groove.

The fifth class comprises cups surrounded by concentric rings and flexed lines.

The sixth class comprises concentric rings without a central cup. An example of this was found at Great Hucklow, in the Peak of Derbyshire, in the form of a slab stone about twenty inches in length and in breadth, which has inscribed upon it seven concentric rings, cut around a common centre, but with no cup. The outer ring is about twenty-two inches in diameter.

The seventh class consists of concentric circular lines of the form of a spiral or volute.* This is the rarest form of circular ring cutting in Great Britain, but it is often found on the incised stones of Ireland and Brittany.

Various as are the markings, it seems evident that they are all somewhat closely allied to each other, " belong to the same archaic school of art, and have a community of character and origin, is proved," says Sir J. Simpson, "by the fact of two, three, or more of them being occasionally found carved together upon the same stones or rocks. For, if in some instances we have the sculpturing entirely of one single type or character, we have in other instances, all, or nearly all, the types appearing in one position. Thus, on the rocks at Auchnabreach, near the Crinan Canal, there are cups both single and ringed, with all kinds of concentric circles and volutes. On the megalithic circle of stones, termed the Calder stones, standing within a few miles of Liverpool, I lately traced out all the different types,—as single and ringed cups, concentric circles of various forms, and volutes."

* These are all described in Simpson's Archaic Sculpturings.

CHAPTER II.

Rock-Markings in Northumberland.

AT a meeting of the Archæological Institute, December 4, 1863, the Rev. Dr. Collingwood Bruce called the attention of those present to an extensive series of drawings by Mr. D. Mossman, representing the incised markings of doubtful import occurring upon rocks in Northumberland, chiefly in the neighbourhoods of Wooler, Doddington, and Old Bewick. "Dr. Bruce exhibited also rubbings and mouldings in gutta percha which he had taken from some of the most remarkable rock markings, consisting chiefly of incised concentric circles traversed in one direction by lines which proceed from a central point or cavity. These curious vestiges were first brought under the notice of archæologists by the Rev. W. Greenwell, of Durham, now President of the Tyneside Club of Antiquaries and Naturalists, a memoir on the subject having been read by him at the Annual Meeting of the Institute at Newcastle, in 1857. A short notice of the numerous markings near Ford, in Northumberland, was shortly after published by Dr. Johnson, of Berwick, in his Natural History of the Northern Borders, from the account communicated by Mr. Greenwell, and accompanied by an engraving from a drawing executed by him, which represents a remarkable rock adjacent to a small entrenchment at Routing Linn, near Doddington. This mysterious subject had subsequently attracted the notice of Sir Gardner Wilkinson, by whom some notices have been given in the Journal of the Archæological Association, vol. xvi, 1860, p. 118. The Duke of Northumberland, a few years after, stimulated further investigations, and personally examined the various places where such markings had been noticed. Numerous vestiges of the same class were brought to light shortly after through his Grace's suggestions, especially by the Rev. W. Proctor, of Doddington, and other residents in that part of Northumberland. Some examples had been discovered on rocks concealed under an accumulation of mould, covered by rank vegetation, and indicating the lapse of many years since these circles had been there traced. The origin of such markings, and the period or race to which they may be assigned, remain, as Dr. Bruce stated, without satisfactory explanation. The

Duke of Northumberland, with the noble patronage of researches into the history and antiquities of his country which he has shown in so remarkable a degree, has directed that representations of all these mysterious traces of the earlier inhabitants of the Northern Marches should be prepared for publication, for the purpose of eliciting information regarding any like vestiges which may occur in any other parts of the British Isles or in foreign countries, and to afford to archæologists accurate materials for investigation of so curious a subject. It is remarkable that, as Dr. Bruce observed, these markings appear to have been produced by a metal implement ; this is shown by indications of tooling in the grooved lines, wrought as if by an iron chisel upon the hard rocks of the Cheviot district."

In the reference made by Sir Gardner Wilkinson, alluded to above, that gentleman said :—" Many other remarkable mementos of our British ancestors might be noticed ; but I shall be satisfied for the present to invite attention to certain rude concentric rings carved upon stones, which, as far as my observations carry me, only occur outside the *enceinte* of ancient forts, or of sacred circles. They appear to be confined to the north of our islands, and chiefly to Northumberland. I have also met with one on the long upright stone outside the sacred circle near Penrith in Cumberland, known by the name of ' Long Meg with her daughters,' but they are not found in Devonshire and Cornwall. They generally consist of three or four concentric rings, the outer one measuring from about seven inches to twenty four in diameter ; the innermost one, or centre, being a single dot, from which a line, more or less straight, runs directly through the successive rings, and extends beyond the circumference of the outermost one. The first that I observed was that on the stone called ' Long Meg,' near Penrith. This was in 1835, at which time, I believe, they had never been noticed ; and though I continued to search for them in many places, it was not till 1850 that in visiting the double British Camp called Old Bewick, in Northumberland, I met with other instances of these concentric rings. I there found several carved upon two large blocks respectively thirty and a hundred and thirteen paces beyond the outermost vallum of that camp.

"Though I had found at length, after so many fruitless inquiries, that the one in Cumberland, was not a solitary instance of this device, I was unable to hear of any more, until, in 1851, the attention of the Archæological Institute, during their meeting at Newcastle, was directed to them by the discovery of others

at Rowting Lynn, near Ford in Northumberland ; and I was grati-
fied by the sight of a copy of them. But nothing was then, nor
has since that time been elicited, to shew their object or their
meaning; and I am not disposed to maintain the opinion which
at first suggested itself to me, that they related to the circular
camps, and certain dispositions connected with them, such as are
traced in times of danger by the Arabs on the sand, to guide the
movements of a force coming to their rescue.

"I afterwards visited those of Routing Lynn also, and found that
the rock on which they were cut, stands, as usual, outside the
camp ; the agger of which is still traceable, though there are
remains of other mounds beyond it, which may have surrounded
the external enclosure in which it stands. The rings are very numerous, amounting to between twenty and thirty ; and the rock is
rather more than seventy feet in length. Some are more varied
in form than those of Old Bewick, though they seem mostly to be
designed on the same principle, with the exception of some small
rings, and one of a semi-elliptical figure. This last measures
twelve inches in breadth and ten in height. The largest of the
other rings are, respectively, of 2 ft. $0\frac{1}{2}$ in., 2 ft., 1 ft. 10 in.,
1 ft. 8 in., and 1 ft. 3 in. diameter.

"On one of the blocks at Old Bewick are about five rings ; and
the other bears from ten to twelve, some of which are double, like
those at Routing Lynn. Other rings are said to be found in Northumberland, at Dowth, and at Fordwestfield ; and another occurs
on a stone in one of the cells of a Tumulus opened in 1853 at
Pickaquoy, near Kirkwall, in Orkney. Some at New Grange, near
Drogheda, in Ireland (on the upright slates forming the entrance-
passage to the sepulchral cell), representing a scroll shaped design,
may be thought to present a similar character ; but others at the
same place, which are convoluted, and consist of several spiral
folds turning in opposite directions, differ essentially from the concentric rings here alluded to ; and are more like those at Gavr
Innis, in the Morbihan. Others are found on what are called the
Calder-Stones, near Liverpool ; but the principal one being convoluted, while two others consist each of a central and outer ring, with
another device below one of them, of elongated and pointed form
like an animal's nose, these may also be considered distinct from
the concentric rings of Northumberland ; though they may assist
in establishing the fact of circular devices having been common in
the northern parts of the country. Those, which are of the very
complicated character before mentioned, bear some analogy to the

mazes or labyrinths met with in Cumberland, Yorkshire, Bedford-shire, Hampshire, Wiltshire, Dorsetshire, and other parts of England, cut in turf, and varying from about thirty to sixty, or a hundred and ten feet, in diameter ; and to others formed of stone which are found in Italy. But it may be doubted whether these mazes bear any relationship to the concentric rings ; and if, as I have before observed, these ring-devices are confined to the north, and are unknown in the south, of England, there is less reason to feel surprise or regret at this circumstance, as it appears to be consistent with the fact of stones inscribed with various emblems being common in Scotland. Indeed, one of those figured in Wilson's Prehistoric Annals of Scotland, which was once the cover-stone of a cist found at at Coilsfield, in Ayrshire, has concentric rings carved upon it, not very unlike some at Routing Lynn and Old Bewick ; and that it is of British time, is proved by the pattern on the urn containing the burnt bones buried in the tomb. There is also one given in plate 123 of Mr. Stuart's Sculptured Stones of Scotland, which was found at High Auchinlay by Wigton Bay, and has similar rings ; though the other sculptured stones contained in that interesting work are of Christian time, and have the western or papal cross ; with the fish, the mirror and comb, and various fanciful devices of a much later period than the pagan era.

"The introduction of emblems such as the concentric rings, in which the monuments of the north differ from those of Devonshire, and Cornwall, and other southern parts of Britain, may be owing to some diversity in the habits of the two peoples ; for though similar in their general customs, and in their erection of sacred circles, cromlechs and other monuments, the Celtic tribes of the north and south had some peculiarities, which may be traced in their tombs and dwellings, and in certain points where a difference might reasonably be expected from their being far removed from each other ; and, above all, from their belonging, in most cases, not merely to different *tribes*, but to two distinct *branches* of the Celtic 'family. It must, however, be admitted that those who lived still further to the south had the custom of engraving stones with various devices ; and some found at Gavr Innis, in the Mor-bihan, are covered with most complicated patterns."*

Mr. Lukis exploring the cromlech at this place, some fifty years ago, found the props covered with engraved lines forming patterns

---

* Jour. Arch. Assoc., 16, p. 118.

resembling the tatooing of the New Zealander. There were also a number of flat stones lying about, which were also engraved. A number of rubbings with heel-ball were taken—as rubbings of monumental brasses are taken, and facsimiles of these may be seen in the Journal of the British Archæological Association, vol. 3, p. 273. The patterns are sunk in the stone about half an inch deep, and though some of them appear to resemble each other, they cannot be said to be attempts at exact imitation.

Attention seems to have been first of all called to the mysterious markings on the rocks of Northumberland, at the annual meeting of the Archæological Institute at Newcastle, in the autumn of 1852, by the Rev. William Greenwell, who read a paper upon the subject, and to whom the credit of bringing so curious a discovery under consideration is due. The resumption of the subject by Sir Gardner Wilkinson in 1860, we have just mentioned. The publicity given to the statements of these gentlemen brought other antiquaries into the field, and information has been supplied relative to such markings found in many parts of England, Scotland, and Ireland. Mr. G. V. Dunoyer, relates that in some of the southern districts of Ireland, the rock surfaces are found to present numerous markings similar to those in the Cheviot district. These have been the subject of careful investigation by Dean Graves of Dublin, who in a memoir to the Royal Irish Academy expressed the opinion that the concentric circles, lines and other singular configurations found upon such incised rocks, represent, although very rudely, fortified dwellings, entrenched works and lines of communication, such as abound in the sister kingdom. Whether this be so or not, it is worthy of remark that the same general supposition regarding those found in Northumberland was entertained by Mr. Greenwell, the first antiquary as before mentioned, who brought the discovery forward, and it is thus stated in the earliest published notice, namely, that communicated by him to Dr. Johnston, of Berwick, by whom it was given, with a reproduction of Mr. Greenwell's drawing of the remarkable rock at Routing Lynn, near Doddington, in the Natural History of the Eastern Borders. The celebrity of this rock induces us to transcribe a short account of it from the pages of Mr. George Tate's pamphlet, "Ancient Sculptured Rocks of Northumberland." He says :—"The great stone at Routing Lynn, though not the first discovered, may be first described, as it is nearly the most northerly in situation, and contains the largest number and greatest variety of inscriptions. It is situate on the edge of wild dreary moor lands, about midway between Doddington and Ford, by the side of a burn, which tumbles over a sandstone cliff some thirty feet in height, into the Lynn (Celtic) a pool at its base. The meaning of the name is pretty well ascertained—*Routing* (from *rout—a*) means to bellow ; and is applied both in Northumberland, and in Scotland to the bellowing of cattle. When the burn is swollen with the rainfall from the hills, it becomes a torrent ; and falling over the cliff into the Lynn, with a loud noise like the routing or bellowing of cattle, it is called the Routing Lynn.

"This rock is the largest of all the inscribed stones discovered ; and yet it is but a fragment, for part of it has been quarried away on the south side ; it is *in situ*, rising 10 feet above the ground on the south side, with a short abrupt slope to the south, and a larger slope towards the north and west : it is 60 feet in length from east to west, and 40 feet in its broadest part. Rising so much above the ground, it is more ridged and irregular in its surface than most other rocks. Untrimmed by art, it is rough as nature has left it, and yet over all parts—over ridges and hollows, as well as over smoother places, the mysterious figures have been incised. How many figures may have been on this rock originally, it is impossible to say ; now, fifty-five are traceable on its northern and western slopes, and five more on its weather-worn and deeply-guttered southern aspect. Doubtless, the whole stone had been covered with inscriptions, and originally there would not be less than one hundred figures.

"Most of the figures are typical forms. One of them has a hook-like process at the side ; here is an arched figure like a recessed Gothic doorway ; here are concentric circles with two and three grooves issuing from them ; here are horse shoe forms, and here is the singular figure with nine radiating grooves from the top of the outer circle. This appendage was first noticed in 1855, when Mr. John Stuart, Secretary of Antiquaries of Scotland, and myself, visited this stone. One outer ray is directed south 20° east, the other south 15° west, and the middle ray, south by east. Some of the compound figures are peculiar ; there is the plant-like form, with its stem, branches, and floral heads ; there are two circles a little apart, united by a groove passing from centre to centre, reminding one of the curious and unexplained spectacle ornament on the Scottish sculptured stones ; and there are other two circles with long tails uniting and ending in cups, and which perchance, might conventionally represent comets.

" The figures on this stone have a more artistic appearance than most others, which is partly due to the care with which they have been formed, and partly to the moulding action of the elements, the incised circles and grooves are deep, usually from one-fourth to three-eighths of an inch ; some are even half an inch ; the hollows or cups are deeper still, some being as deep as one inch and a half. In size, the figures range from three inches to two feet nine inches in diameter ; the common size is fiteen inches.   Twelve years ago, the lower part of the stone was concealed by a covering of peat nine inches in depth.

" This marvellous rock is within an ancient British camp, which occupies an angle formed by the bend of the Routing Lynn Burn, and is defended on the north and west sides partly by deep gullies, and on the other by four strong rampiers and ditches.   Like some other camps of the same age, it has attached to it a large area enclosed by a supplemental rampier, and it is within this area, about midway between the camp and the external rampier, that the inscribed rock stands.

" This part of Northumberland appears to be particularly rich in these incomprehensible markings, for within a distance of twelve or fifteen miles,—between Routing Lynn and Beanley Moor—between forty and fifty sculptured rocks have been discovered, with more than three hundred examples of rings and concentric circles cut upon them.   As far back as 1825, Mr. Langlands, of Old Bewick, noticed one of these sculptured rocks ; but it was the Mr. Greenwell of Durham, whom we have already mentioned, who in 1852 first called public attention to them, and commenced the inquiry which afterwards yielded so much information.   He, indeed, was the discoverer of the celebrated rock at Routing Lynn.   He did this quite accidently one day when he happened to be resting near the locality.   A part of the rock happened to be exposed, and he fancied he noticed some appearance of carving upon it.   Of course such an enthusiastic and accomplished archæologist at once took steps to satisfy his curiosity, by removing from the surface of the rock, portions of its thick and ancient covering of turf.   His search was speedily rewarded by the discovery of those wonderful markings we have just been describing, an account of which he read at the Archæological Institute's meeting at Newcastle in 1852.   The paper, however, was unfortunately lost, and consequently is not to be found in their printed Transactions.

" It will be interesting to add here a short extract from Dr. John-ston's ' Natural History of the Eastern Borders,' which we have said, was one of the earliest works to notice and describe this marvellous rock. He is speaking of the Osmunda Regalis (the Royal Fern) as being found on the water ledge above the Routing Lynn, and then he says :—'The burn now hurries down a deep woody glen ; and almost immediately leaps the much higher and more beautiful lynn—the Routing-Lynn. This is an attractive scene, richly embowered with wood, and covered with every gift that our northern Flora deemed suitable to its adornment ;—but we must re-ascend, for we have passed unnoticed some things worthy of a note. About 50 yards above the first lynn, the sides of the burn heave on each side with mounds and parallel fosses, that have evidently an artificial origin, and that in a far-away time. They are green with sward, and too imperfect to permit their plan to be restored ; but it has been conjectured that they are the traces of what had been strongholds and encampments of the Danes,—the savage warriors of the far Norrowaie. From the remains, it has been also inferred that the encampment must have been extensive and intended for permanency. A little apart, on the south, there juts above the level of the moor a rounded sandstone rock. The scalp of this rock is about 20 feet across, concave, rather smooth, irregularly cracked, and with even spaces ; and these are engraved all over with figures, each consisting of a series of grooved rings, often dotted in the bottom of the grooves. The figures are scattered, and vary in size, the largest being little more than a foot in diameter, but they are alike in form and in sculpture. Short parallel lines lead away, for a few inches, from some of them ; but no two circles appear to have been connected.

"Such is the spot ; and I wish that I could penetrate the mysstery of its history. Some portion is easily read. Long—long ago, the bog was a lake. Thither the Red Deer and the Roes of the wide moor, and the White cattle of the forest came to drink, and, in the encircling wood, to find shelter from the fervour of the summer sun. The Osmunda probably grew abundantly in this wood. Centuries came and went, and each marked its reign by usurpations on the water, until what was lake became a swamp,—a bog,—and a wooded basin ;—such is the force and sure result of unchecked vegetation. When a lake, the burn that relieved it from an overflow was much more considerable than that which now is ; and it may have been the impassable lake behind, and the plentiful supply of water it furnished, that led the northern invaders to select this locality for the site of their Camp. In front the precipices of the lynns were good defence ; and thence the warder's eye could scan the country all around. Presuming the

erections to have been Danish, we may date their foundation some-
where about the year 870, when 'King Healfdene reigned in Nor-
thumbria'; and seventy years and five afterwards, the camp was
wrested from the conquerors in one of the most memorable battles
on record." Dr. Johnston here digresses a little to introduce an
account of this battle. This is taken from the Historia Anglorum
of Henry of Huntingdon. "In the year of grace 945, and in the
fourth year of his reign, King Athelstan fought at Brunesburh,
one of the greatest battles on record against Anlaf, King of Ireland, who had united his forces to those of the Scots and Danes
settled in England. Of the grandeur of this conflict, English
writers have expatiated in a sort of poetical description, in which
they have employed both foreign words and metaphors. I therefore give a faithful version of it, in order that, by translating their
recital almost word for word the majesty of the language may
exhibit the majestic achievements and the heroism of the English
nation.

"'At Brunesburh, Athelstan the king, noblest of chiefs, giver of
collars, emblems of honour, with his brother Edmund, of a race
ancient and illustrious, in the battle, smote with the edge of the
sword. The offspring of Edward, the departed king, cleft through
the defence of shields, struck down noble wariors. Their innate
valour, derived from their fathers, defended their country, its
treasures and its hearths, its wealth and its precious things, from
hostile nations, in constant wars. The nation of the Irish, and
the men of ships, rushed to the mortal fight; the hills re-echoed
their shouts. The warriors struggled from the rising of the sun,
illuminating depths with its cheerful rays, the candle of God, the
torch of the Creator, till the hour when the glorious orb sunk in
the west. There numbers fell, Danish by race, transfixed with
spears, pierced through their shields; and with them fell the
Scottish men, weary and war sad. But chosen bands of the West
Saxons, the live-long day, unshrinking from toil, struck down the
ranks of their barbarous foe; men of high breeding handled the
spear, Mercian men hurled their sharp darts. There was no safety
to those who with Anlaf, coming over the sea, made for the land
in wooden ships, fated to die. Five noble kings, fell on the field,
in the prime of their youth, pierced with the sword; seven earls
of King Anlaf, and Scots without number. Then were the Northmen quelled in their pride. For not a few came over the sea to
the contest of war; while but a few heard their king's groans, as
borne on the waves, he fled from the rout. Then was fierce Froda,

chief of the Northmen, Constantine with him, King of the Scots, stayed in his boasting, when corpses were strewed on that battle-field, sad remnant left of kindred bands, relatives and friends, mixed with the common folk slain in the fight; there, too, his dear son was stretched on the plain, mangled with wounds. Nor could Danish Gude, hoary in wisdom, soft in his words, boast any longer. Nor could Anlaf himself, with the wreck of his troops, vaunt of success in the conflicts of war, in the crashing of spears, in crossing of swords, in councils of wise men. Mothers and nurses wailed for their dear ones, playing the game of ill-fated war with the sons of King Edward.

" 'The Northmen departed in their nailed barks, and Anlaf, defeated, over the deep sought his own land, sorrowing much. Then the two brothers Wessex regained, leaving behind them relics of war, the flesh of the slain, a bloody prey. Now the black raven with crooked beak, the livid toad, and eagle and kite, the dog and the wolf, with tawny hide, gorged themselves freely on the rich feast. No battle ever was fought in this land so fierce and so bloody, since the time that came hither, over the broad sea, Saxons and Angles, the Britons to rout; famous war-smiths, who struck down the Welsh, defeated their nobles, seized on the land.

"C.—That is not exactly a Wellington dispatch? S.—No, nor much to the purpose! 'Bruneburh here or Bruneburh there,'—*there* certainly was once a camp, and I think that the circles we lie upon were made by the soldiers of that camp in relief of idle-ness. They would be basking here, like bees in the sun. A.—Pooh! that explanation won't do: it will not explain wherefore the figures are all uniform and circular: soldier's fancies do not run in one vein. S.—True,—but there was a model to guide them in their work—they were like children, making a plan of their camp below,—and each trying to excel his neighbour in exactness. A.—A mere get off! Danish camps were not circular, at least not this one; they were earthen mounds thrown up to aid a natural defence, or to give a vantage-point of offence. I cannot but be-lieve that on the rock before us, we have engraved a plan, or rude map of the camp of the district which belonged to the aboriginal Britons. From the rock there is a distinct view of the entire Cheviot range, and, on almost every hill-top of them, was once a circular camp, wherein every tribe sheltered themselves from hos-tile attacks, and whence they issued on a foray. A tribe, pitched where we are standing, would overlook and watch every move-ment; and it is natural enough to conclude that some one amongst them, with a taste for the art, might have indulged his skill in making this sketch,—the circles being made to vary in size according to the variation of the camps on the opposed hills. This conjecture, I believe, has suggested itself to others who have examined the rock,—and in special to the Rev. W. Greenwell—and it receives confirmation from the discovery of another rock, with sculptures of the same character, not above ten miles southwards—viz., near unto Bewick.

"Scarcely a mile from Routing Lynn is Hunter's Moor; here also is an inscribed rock of considerable size, and bearing figures somewhat different to those found in other localities. Most of them are of the usual type, but others are curiously united by straight and curved grooves. We have in one place a group of four concentric circles, and right across their diameters runs a groove connecting them with other combined figures. In another place is an irregular, rounded, angular figure, enclosing two hollows or cups, and united with a broad oval figure. Another, around four cups approaches to the reniform. A very similar stone to this is found at Stonehaven in Scotland, apparently belonging to the same family and age, from the fact that it has the peculiar cups, circles and combinations to be found in the Hunter's Moor Rock, without any of the ordinary typical figures. The latter rock has figures as large as 28 inches in diameter. In its neighbourhood are other rocks abounding with inscriptions which for the most part have become defaced by time and other causes; here there are concentric circles 30 inches in diameter."

Another stone, described as far more important than any of these, was discovered by Mr. Greenwell, in the shape of a cist cover, at Ford West Field, about a mile westward of Routing Lynn; on this were cut three incomplete concentric circles round a cup; of course the circles may have been originally complete.

In the Doddington district, rock inscriptions literally abound, no less than twenty-five stones have been discovered by the Rev. William Procter and members of his family, while other historic remains are found on the same moors in similar profusion.

Miss Procter had the honour and pleasure of discovering in 1859, one of the most curious of these inscribed stones. It lay in a cultivated field called the High Chesters, covered with turf, as deep in some places as twelve inches. Owing to this, the markings had been most remarkably preserved from the action of the weather and other destructive agencies, and they were almost as fresh as when the hand of man produced them; it is therefore one of the most important rocks as shewing well the character of primæval work. It is thus described by Mr. George Tate :—" It juts out from the hillside—an irregular mass—ridged and broken on the surface, sloping more or less in all directions, but chiefly towards the west ; the whole surface, which is 9 feet long by 7 feet broad, is crowded with figures, chiefly of the ordinary type of concentric circles, some of which are grouped into compound figures by grooves. Here there are oval, horse-shoe, and pear-shaped figures. One form is very peculiar ; a circle around a cup, and with two hook-like grooves from one side of the circle. Very rude are both the shape and workmanship of the figures ; many of the incisions are shallow, still retaining distinct marks of the blunt tools by which the rock had, with little skill been chipped away. Some of the hollows are, however, wide and deep. Thirty figures are traceable on this stone."

" Proceeding on through Harelaw, Horton, and Dod Law, we find in all directions similar examples of rocks with their cuttings of rings and cups, the honours of discovery apparently being shared by the Procter family throughout. Thirty yards eastward of the Ringses Camp, Mrs. Procter discovered a stone differing considerably in its markings from all others. Its figures are rude irregular squares ; one of them with three incomplete concentric squares around fourteen hollows, from one of which proceeds a groove to another cup, and then away through an opening in the squares to the extremity of the stone. Another single quadrangular figure encloses eight cups, and has a groove passing through, but forked at its commencement and starting from two different cups. An analogous figure approaches to a heart shape. Imaginative speculators, might in these figures find countenance to the notion of the inscriptions being plans of camps ; for here we could fancy there were camps with one and three rampiers. A gateway through them—hut dwellings scattered over the area enclosed, and a hollow way leading out of the camp. The shape however of the imaginary camp does not correspond with those of the period. So different are these figures from other inscriptions, that they might have been referred to a different age and people ; but their association with other figures of the normal types, shews their common origin. Three other groups of figures, curved and of irregular forms, are on the scalp of the same rock, but at some distance from each other. Like as with others, this rock was covered over with turf till 1855, when it was discovered by Mrs. Procter, who at once had part of it cleared, and ultimately further portions, exposing an area of 16 feet by 8 feet covered with figures." *

* Tate's Ancient Rocks.

The lady mentioned above (Mrs. Procter) had the good fortune to discover other incised rocks in the same part of the country as those we have been describing. " On Glod Law, a platform of rock breaking out of the south-west encampment of Dod Law, and ranging from north-west to south-east, seven groups of inscriptions have been discovered. In this assemblage of sculptures, there are traceable thirty six figures, mostly typical forms ; yet in some cases so varied and combined, as to present new figures."

The most remarkable of the groups was that discovered by Mrs. Procter, and is thus described by Mr. Tate. " In this group there are two series of large concentric circles attached to each other ; one, consisting of six circles, 26 inches in diameter ; the other, the largest figure discovered, being 39 inches in diameter, and having eight complete concentric circles and part of another. In this large figure there are the central cup and three radial grooves, none of which, however, extends to the centre, but two of them start from the circumference of the innermost circle, and the other from the second circle. There is no other example of three radial grooves. The whole of the sculptures are rudely formed, the incisions are shallow, and the tool marks distinct ; the circles are irregular, and had evidently been drawn without instrumental aid. A short distance from them, Mrs. Procter afterwards discovered the fragments of a sepulchral urn of the ordinary ancient British type."

Southward of the foregoing—about two miles, is Whitsunbank. There is a lofty hill on which are eight different inscribed stones, all of which were discovered by Mr. George Tate and Mr. William Wightman.   Thirty-two figures are clearly traceable on these rocks.

" On the summit of the hill on a tolerable smooth surface of rock, which has a gentle slope to the north, there are seven figures all typical. The largest figure of six circles is bulged out in breadth ; from east to west it is 24 inches in diameter ; but only 21 inches from north to south ; it is connected by a long wavy groove with another group of concentric circles of similar proportions. The union in this case is from centre to centre ; but two other groups are united by a straight groove from the centre of the one to the circumference of the other group."

About the same hill are other inscriptions most of which are very much defaced. One in particular is considered specially interesting, because of its being near to an ancient British cist of an extremely rude form, cut out of the rock, in which were found the calcined bones of a human skeleton, and a flint arrow head, which had been subject to the action of fire. Several other tumuli are also found on the same hill.

There is another curious stone, discovered in 1860, on a hill over looking Coldmartin Lough, with a rough, broken and jagged surface, on which thirteen figures are traceable—some pear-shaped, with two and three grooves issuing from the circles. Mr. Tate contends that the rugged, irregular, and steeply sloping surfaces of this rock and of that at High Chesters, completely dissipate the fancy entertained by some, that the sculptures were used for games, since no games could be played on such uneven and inclined surfaces.

"This assemblage of inscriptions at first sight appeared exceptional, as to their associations; but further research has shown, not only that they are near to ancient graves, but also not far distant from ancient British camps. On the north side of the hill is the Weetwood Camp, in which were found a quern made of porphyry, a stone trough, similar in appearance to the pot querns found in Ireland, and three round stone balls artificially formed, about 3 inches in diameter, which it has been supposed were used for some game. More distinctive are the camps found on the south side of the hill; no less than five are within a distance of a quarter to half a mile; the nearest is a large double camp; the others are very simple in form, being circular and formed of a single rampart of stone, earth and sods; the rampier of the Fowberry Camp, which is small, has a thickness of 9 feet. Near to one of these camps are traces of several hut circles, showing that there had been one or more ancient British villages on the slope of the hill." *

On Chatton Law, four miles from Whitsunbank, where are the remains of an ancient British Camp of about half an acre in extent, is a sandstone rock, on which in 1859 Mr. H. Mac Lauchland discovered inscribed stones.

Within the camp is one of the engraved stones, containing six figures of the common type, but outside—some 200 yards eastward—a large mass of sandstone has been discovered abounding in sculptures, some of which are remarkably large. One is 36 inches in diameter, and composed of seven concentric rings with a peculiar curved crown at the top. "From its central hollow, issues a long wavy groove which had linked together other forms now obliterated;

* Tate on Sculptured Rocks.

one, however, still remaining of four concentric circles attached to the groove by a branch.   Those who fancy that these inscriptions symbolise the progress of life, might imagine the smaller circles to be germinations from the larger ; similarly as life among zoophytes is generated by buds or gemmules issuing from the old parents." *

In the vicinity is also a concentric oval, with two grooves proceeding from the outer figure.

The Law is surrounded by ancient British remains, no less than six other camps, very ancient indeed, can be seen, and near one of them a bronze leaf-shaped sword was found.

* Tate

CHAPTER III.

Rock Markings in Yorkshire.

ILKLEY in Yorkshire is one of the most conspicuous of British localities for curious and interesting rock markings, a few of which we now proceed to describe. The town occupies the site of the Roman station of Olicana, on the banks of the river Wharfe. Behind the town is Rumbold's Moor, a wilderness of rock and heather, part of which is 1322 feet above the level of the sea. Below this moor extend some four or five miles of rugged cliffs in a direction nearly due east and west; here most of the sculptured rocks are found, at heights varying from 800 to 1,000 feet above sea level. It has been said that in studying these inscriptions, the grandeur of the scenery about Wharfedale should always be borne in mind, "the cuttings perhaps having been connected with religious observances, of which Nature worship formed a part."

"The geological formation of the district is millstone grit, cropping up from the surrounding heath in huge rocks, blackened by age, and assuming all kinds of strange weird shapes, which, when seen from a distance through the mists so common on these moors, are well calculated to inspire the superstitions with awe, even in the prosaic nineteenth century. Some of the names of the rocks are remarkable, and deserve notice ; for instance, the Noon Stone, the Sepulchral Stone, the Doublers, etc."

Here we find a good many interesting specimens of incised rocks, to a few of which we may make brief allusion. Near what is called the Panorama Rock, a mile south-west of Ilkley, and from the summit of which, 800 feet above the sea level, a splendid view of the surrounding country can be obtained, are several of the finest specimens of the sculptured stones. For years these had been covered up completely with turf, and it was not till this had been cleared away, that the inscriptions, which owed their preservation to this agency, were brought to light. One stone measures 10 feet by 7 feet, and is almost entirely embedded in the ground where it lies. It is marked with twenty-five cups, eighteen of which are surrounded with concentric rings, varying from one to five in number. The rings are intersected and joined together by some ladder shaped grooves of so remarkable a character, that Mr. Allen says

c 2

ho does not think this peculiar type of carving occurs anywhere else besides near Ilkley.

Another stone measures 15 ft. by 12 ft., and supports a smaller one of triangular shape, 6 ft. by 4 ft. They are both carved with cups and rings, but exposure to the atmosphere has caused considerable damage to the markings. The upper stone has eleven cups, two of which are surrounded by single rings, and the under stone has forty-two cups, nine of which have rings. A third stone measuring 10 ft. by 9 ft., has twenty-seven cups, fourteen of which have concentric rings around them. Some other stones in the neighbourhood have cup marks without rings. Amongst the forty-two cups on the stone mentioned above are some unusually fine examples, one oval cup being five inches by four inches, surrounded by two rings, the diameter of the outer ring being one foot three inches.

A mile south-east of Ilkley railway station, are the Cow and Calf Rocks, two enormous masses of grit-stone, which have fallen from the cliffs above. Near these rocks a part of the cliff has a group of twenty-five cups, of diameters varying from 1 to 3 inches. Seven of the cups have around them incomplete rings, and many are connected by an arrangement of grooves. The rock is very hard, and the cuttings are extremely rude and imperfect in their execution.

Higher up the moor, south of the Cow and Calf Rocks, near the Pancake Ridge, is an extensive mass of grit stone, 15 ft. long, by 11 ft. 6 in. broad, by 5 ft. 6 in. high, on which are cut between 40 and 50 cups, some of which are surrounded by single concentric rings, but there are no connecting grooves.

Near the Ilkley Baths—about the eighth of a mile south-west, is a stone 7 ft. 6 in. long by 6 ft. broad and 2 ft. high, on which are marked 13 cups, 6 of which are surrounded by rings. Near Graining's Head, a mile and a quarter south of Ilkley, is a large block of grit-stone, 12 ft. by 7 ft. 6 in. by 4 ft.: on this are carved about fifty cups, sixteen of which are surrounded with single concentric rings, and here is one of the very few instances in which cup and ring marks are found on the vertical surface of a rock.

Near the Addingham high moor, by the valley of the Wharfe, is a large block of stone 19 ft. long, by 7 ft. broad, by 4 ft. 6 in. thick, of considerable interest and celebrity, owing to the resemblance of its markings to those on the stone at Tossene, on the coast of Sweden, as we have described elsewhere in our notice of Holmberg's *Skandinavien's Hallristningar.*

There is another of these stones near Addingham Crag, on which are cut twenty-three cups.

Three years after Mr. J. R. Allen had brought under the notice of the British Archæological Association his interesting notes upon the sculptured rocks of Ilkley, he again communicated with that body, and in a paper read in March, 1882, supplied a number of further particulars illustrative of the same locality. Amongst those he then mentioned were the Doubler Stones, situated on Rumbold's Moor, three miles south-south-west of Ilkley, and two miles east of Silsden. "These rocks," he says, "are by far the most remarkable freaks of nature to be seen in the district. They occupy a prominent position, perched on the extremity of a rocky knoll which juts out into the valley; and as seen from below, with their weird forms standing out clear and sharp against the back-ground of blue sky, they present so extraordinary an appearance that they would at once attract the attention of even the most unobservant. In general outline they resemble gigantic toadstools; and I presume that they are called the Doubler Stones from the fact of their shapes being almost identical. They may be appropriately described as Nature's twins. The upper surface of the cap of one of these stones has three large basin-shaped cavities in it. Two of these lie along the central axis of the stone, and measure respectively 1 ft. 3 in. by 2 ft. 9 in. deep, and 1 ft. 9 in. by 1 ft. 3 in. by 9 in. deep. They are united by a deep groove, a continuation of which runs out over the edge of the stone at each end. There is another basin lying to the west side of the two central ones, with one of which it is connected by grooves. It measures 2 ft. by 1 ft. 9 in. and is 9 in. deep. There is no direct evidence that these basins are artificial; but it is quite possible that they may have been so originally, and have been enlarged by natural agencies. But in addition to the basins, are twenty-six cup markings of distinctly artificial origin. They vary in diameter from 2 to 4 in. One group of cups appears to be arranged in a series of parallel rows. The other stone has no basins on its upper surface, but eight cup markings can be counted."

Near Piper's Crag is a rock surface in a horizontal position on a portion of which, 7 ft. by 5 ft., are found 15 cups of 2 and 3 in. diameter. One is surrounded by a single ring, four by a double ring, and one by a triple ring.

There is also the stone on Weary Hill, about a mile south-west of Ilkley, a boulder of grit-stone, measuring 8 ft. by 5 ft. It bears on its upper surface ten cups, varying from 2 to 3 in. In the same neighbourhood is the " Neb Stone," which is also cup-marked.

The Pancake Ridge has been alluded to on another page, a mile and a half south-east of Ilkley, south of the celebrated Ben Rhydding Hydropathic Establishment. On the top of the cliff is the large flat grit-stone slab, called from its peculiar shape the " Pancake Rock." Mr. Allen says, " On its upper surface are several cup markings much obliterated by the action of the weather, but some of them sufficiently distinct to prove their origin artificial, and to show that this rock was noticed in ancient times, and very possibly considered an object either of worship or superstition. About 150 yards to the west of this Pancake Rock, close to the edge of the cliff, and at a level of 1,010 feet above the sea, is a piece of grit-stone, measuring 5 ft. 3 in. by 5 ft., and 1 ft. 9 in. high. On its upper surface, which is nearly horizontal, are carved thirteen cups, varying in diameter from 2 to 2½ in., eleven of which are surrounded by rings. There is also an elaborate arrangement of connecting grooves. There are also some other stones at the foot of Green Crag, and elsewhere, marked with cups, rings, and grooves as those already described."

In the summer of 1879, Mr. C. W. Dymond, of the British Archæological Association, while rambling over the moors of Yorkshire, discovered on that part of Rumbold's Moor called Burley Moor, a stone marked with what he describes as a very striking group of cups, and which he is of opinion had hitherto escaped observation. It lay alone near the foot of a steep slope, a few minutes walk from the ruins of a small stone circle, which crowns the crest of the pass leading south-south-east from Ilkley to Eldwick, and just a mile and a quarter from the first. The stone is 9 ft. 6 in. in length, 6 ft. 3 in. in breadth, and about 2 ft. in thickness. Upon it were found a number of small cups, which, Mr. Dymond observed could easily be executed by one sitting on that part of the stone which is to the north-west of them. " They assume the form of a band of coupled cups crossing an irregular and incomplete ring of the same, outside which are two small detached groups of four. The whole design seems to belong to that order of cup markings which appear to be arranged with some regard to regularity."

" The first impression conveyed to my mind," says Mr. Dymond, " was that here we may have a rude attempt to pourtray the starry heavens spanned by the galaxy ; and that the outlying groups may have been intended to represent two of the constellations—perhaps Orion, and another not so easily identified. Nor have farther reflexion and inquiry yet suggested a better hypothesis. The relative positions of the cups do not appear generally to correspond with those of chief stars in the visible firmament : nor is it likely that these would be thus mapped with any approach to correctness, when observations, unless retained in the memory, must needs be recorded on the stone in the darkness of the night. The key to the meaning of this, as well as of all other such engravings in the same district, is the more likely to be found as they are studied together ; and thus the discovery of one with new characteristics may possibly throw additional light on this obscure subject. Many parallel instances of the wide spread use of such devices, particularly in ancient times, have been referred to by Mr. J. R. Allen in his compact and valuable paper on the Ilkley rock sculptures ; and indeed, one can hardly open an illustrated book descriptive of the art of a remote past, without finding examples of ornament having much resemblance to, if not identity with these, and strongly suggesting that they had a common origin."

Some months after communicating the above to the British Archæological Association, Mr. Dymond wrote :—" Since my paper on this subject (cup markings on Burley Moor) was published, Mr. J. F. Nichols, of Bristol, has written to me, remarking that he detects in the group of cups, viewed from the indicated point, the outline of a duck or goose. The resemblance had also struck me ; but not being able to call to my mind any instance in which the artist of the rude stone times had represented animal or other object forms in dotted outline, I concluded that the likeness to a bird, though very remarkable, was only accidental. But now, as another antiquary has independently noted the similitude, and is disposed to accept it as the key to the draughtsman's meaning, it may be well to throw the suggestion before others."

In Mr. Ord's History and Antiquities of Cleveland we have an interesting account of the opening of two fine tumuli on Bernaldby Moor, near Eston Nab, in the month of November, 1843. The opening of tumulus number two is thus described :—" Although precisely similar in external form and dimensions to its venerable neighbour, in all internal features it was essentially different. Brown or black loamy earth, fine and powdery, mixed with masses of pure charcoal in dense layers, seemingly of oak, small red burnt stones, and portions of human bones, were alternately thrown up by the workmen, and in this manner our labours progressed till dusk. In this case the men reversed their mode of proceeding, digging a tunnel shaped passage direct east and west through the centre of the tu-

mulus. We had now gone through the middle line, and were about
to relinquish the task in despair, when a lad who was plying vigor-
ously with his spade, cried out, ' Dom it, here's a bit o' carved
stean !' and was on the point of aiming a final *et tu Brute* blow
at the precious relic, when the narrator leaped down, and arrested
the fatal stroke. On examining the place, I found the outline of
a noble urn-shaped vessel, standing upright, covered with a large
shield shaped stone, curiously carved in the interior with some
metallic instrument, representing, as I conceived, either a rude
armorial bearing, or a religious device. With great care, and some
difficulty, I worked round the urn with a knife, detaching it
gradually from the adjacent mould, and having at length fairly
disengaged it from the surrounding mass, held it aloft to the de-
lighted assemblage, who hailed the long expected sarcophagus
with acclamations.

"The largest circumference of the urn is 40 inches, the circumference of the top, 36 inches, height from the base to the
rim, 13 inches, from the rim to the top, $3\frac{1}{2}$ inches. Inside we
found a quantity of calcined bones, comprising portions of the
frontal, temporal, and parietal bones, etc., besides a great many
teeth in a remarkable state of preservation.

" That these barrows were the tombs of men eminent for lofty
station, or distinguished valour, is apparent from the enormous
labour and elaborate design of their formation; and their near
proximity to the celebrated camp at Eston Nab, is additional tes-
timony. That they were Britons is clear from the structure and
rude finish of the lid of the urn, of the urn itself, and the composition of the tumuli. The statements of Camden, of Sir Richard
Colt Hoare, and Mr. Gage, are quite satisfactory as to their British Origin. Nor less authoritative is the decision of Dr. Young,
the historian of Whitby, who says :—' It is certain, by far the
greater part of our houes have been raised by the ancient Britons,
both because there is no other people to whom they can be ascribed,
and because they are found in connection with other antiquities
evidently British. They are the tombs of our rude, but warlike
ancestors ; and many of them must have been erected at the distance of more than two thousand years.'

"The markings on the above stone are certainly very remarkable,
and seem to defy all attempts at explanation. With the exception
of two (which are parallel) the grooves cut in this stone form
angles, acute or obtuse, somewhat of a zigzag pattern."

CHAPTER IV

Rock Markings in Ireland.

A WRITER in the Kilkenny Archæological Journal (Mr. F. Wakeman) remarked a few years ago that it was not too much to say that all over Ireland could be seen archaic rock markings, the character and intention of which antiquaries have not yet fathomed.

Irish examples he described as consisting of two leading varieties, viz.:—(1) Circular hollows, more or less deep, and of a diameter varying in different instances from about 1 ft. 4 in. to 1 in., sometimes found singly, but more usually in groups, and not unfrequently accompanied by incised lines of considerable depth. (2) "Scorings" in wonderful variety, such as are found on the walls of sepulchral carns, as at Dowth, and Newgrange, near Drogheda, at Sliabh-na-Caillighe, Co. Meath, and in the lettered caves of Knockmore, Co. Fermanagh, often comprising characters well formed, carefully cut or punched on the rock or stone, and presenting the appearance of an inscription legible to all who might possess the necessary key.

With regard to Fermanagh, Mr. Wakeman states that all the cup hollows and other markings which he has observed, have been executed upon hard red sandstone, and that in almost every instance the indentations of the pick or other instrument by which they were formed are still distinctly traceable. He affirms that they could not possibly have anything to do with geological phenomena, that they are certainly the work of man; and in their general distribution and constant analogy of design must have been executed with some fixed intention, very well understood at the date of their formation.

The Drumnakilly Cup Markings are found on stones measuring respectively 14 in. by 11 in., and 10 in. by 6 in., and formed part of a floor of a cist containing a very splendid burial urn, placed mouth downwards, and full of calcined human bones. Two other cupped stones, supporting urns, were found in the same cemetery. All the hollows, Mr. Wakeman asserts, are the work of man, and exhibit the marks of the pick by which they were fashioned; he states also that he believes these present the only instance on record of a proved connexion between these cup markings and primitive sepulchral rites.

In the townland of Killibeg, Co. Fermanagh, about three miles from the village of Garrison, are several "Giants' Graves," or "Druids' Altars," as they are sometimes called, all of which have been robbed of their covering 'stones; also a number of Dallans bearing no inscriptions. One of these, however, called Fion Mac Camhal's finger-stone, is said to bear all the appearance of being a primitive monument. The material is red sand-stone, and it now stands above ground 22 in., its breath being 22½ in. at the widest part. This stone has three artificial depressions, one 3½ inches in diameter, another 4 in., and the third a trifle smaller, and is supposed to have some connexion with St. Aidan, but the tradition has been almost entirely lost.

At Drumlion, a mile and a quarter from Enniskillen on the road to Ballyshannon, lies partly buried in the sand, a very fine specimen of these cup-marked stones. About 3 ft. 3 in. by 4 ft. 2 in. are above the ground, and upon the surface are twelve cups, each about 3 in. in diameter, and of varying depths.

Mr. Wakeman, fearing that this stone might be used by the country folk for some gateway or paving purpose, begged it of the owners of the land on which it was found, and then presented it to the Museum of the Royal Irish Academy, where it may now be seen. He describes the cups as most certainly artificial.

Passing on to the townland of Ryfad, at least six large blocks of sandstone are found, five of which are cup marked; four out of the five have concentric rings in addition to the cups.

All who have taken the trouble to make any enquiries into the matter we are now discussing, must have been struck again and again with the plentiful number of these inscribed rocks, to be found in almost every quarter of the globe: it is more than probable that they were once still more numerous, for it is positively known that in many localities they have either been broken up to mend the roads, or have been utilised in various ways for building and other purposes. One of these stones at Ryfad had been severely maltreated by certain persons who were anxious to ascertain to what practical use their material could be applied. According to the account given of this attempt by an eye-witness, the stone was so hard that the chisels instead of penetrating it, "hopped off like shot"; it is said also that the mysterious markings roused the superstitious fears of the despoilers, and induced them the more readily to abandon their attempts.

Some years ago when the subject of rock markings was comparatively new to the public, Dean Graves (afterwards Bishop of Limerick) made a communication of considerable interest to the Royal Irish Academy, of which he was then President, and which was deemed of sufficient importance to reprint in the Journal of the Kilkenny Archæological Society.

He tells us that his attention was first directed to them by the late Mr. Richard Hitchcock, who in the year 1848, had made some drawings of certain rocks he had lately met with in Ireland, when searching under Dean Graves's direction for Ogham inscriptions in the county of Kerry. In 1851, the Dean saw those monuments himself. He says :—" In that year, in company with the Earl of Dunraven, I traversed a great part of Kerry, with the view of examining all the Ogham inscriptions of whose existence I had been informed, and in the hope of discovering others. 1 had then, in the course of a minute and leisurely survey, opportunities of observing the objects of antiquarian interest, which abound in that picturesque and primitive region. After visiting the very remarkable structure named Staigue Fort, near West-cove, on the Kenmare river, we were led by Mr. Jermyn, of Castle Cove House, to see an inscribed rock, about a mile to the south of the rock, and close to Staigue bridge. He informed us that a large portion of the rock having been stripped about forty years before of the turf by which it had been covered to a depth of three or four feet, was found to be inscribed with circles, single and concentric, shallow circular hollows, small dots and lines. The information previously supplied by Mr. Hitchcock, prepared us for what we were to see. Nevertheless, we were surprised when the vast extent of surface covered by these strange markings was presented to our view ; and we could not help wondering that so curious an object should have excited so little attention. Our first task was to make a heel-ball rubbing of the portion of the rock covered by the most remarkable group of circles. We then made a complete map of the whole rock, and roughly laid down the positions of the outlying circles and lines. This map shews that the incised lines and circles occupy a space of many square yards. The rock itself is of the coarse slate which prevails in the surrounding district, the portion on which the inscriptions occur presenting a very irregular surface. The incised lines are from one quarter to one third of an inch deep, and from half to three-quarters of an inch broad. They are rudely executed, and appear to have been formed by repeated vertical blows, and not by means of a cutting tool held obliquely, and driven by a mallet. This mode of execution characterises all the most ancient inscriptions which I have seen in Ireland ; such, for instance, as the spiral lines and other patterns on the walls and roofs of the chambers in the mound of New Grange, and the strokes in the oldest Oghams. The circular hollows are, in general, about two inches in diameter, and vary in depth from half an inch to an inch.

" In the hope of discovering other markings of the same kind, we procured the assistance of some labourers, and stripped a portion of the rock at a considerable distance from the principal group of circles. This experiment was successful. It led to the discovery of three circles, which had previously been covered by turf three feet in thickness. These latter appeared better preserved than some of those traced on the already exposed parts of the stone.

" The inscriptions of this kind which I have next to mention were discovered by Lord Dunraven and myself, near Ballynasane bridge, about six miles to the east of Dingle. They are two in number, and like those at Staigue bridge, are cut upon the surface of the natural rock. They present, however, distinctive features which deserve notice. Whilst all the circles on the rock at Staigue are perfect, several of those at Ballynasane are incomplete. Sometimes a short and slightly curved line, drawn from a small hollow outside the circle to the central cup, passes through the open part of the circumference. More frequently, this line stops short just as it reaches the break in the circle.

The inscriptions which remain to be noticed are distinguished by the circumstance that they are found on detached stones, of different sizes. The most remarkable of them was discovered by Mr. Hitchcock in 1848, at Aghacarrible, not far from Ballynasane. It is cut on a large stone, which appears to have formerly stood erect, but which now rests in an oblique position, leaning against, and partly imbedded in, a fence.

[The markings on this stone are nearly all a series of concentric rings surrounding a central cup.]

" It is deserving of notice, that in the immediate neighbourhood are many ancient remains of various kinds—standing stones, forts, and caves. In one of the latter are three Ogham inscriptions, and two incised crosses of a peculiar and primitive form.

" In the neighbouring townland of Gowlane, Mr. Hitchcock found three stones. All of these are of a similar character, viz , concentric rings surrounding cups.

" In 1854, the rector of the parish of Kilcrohane, county of Kerry, informed me of the existence of one of these inscribed stones at Tullakeel, about two miles from Sneem. The monument is a large stone, forming part of a modern fence. The principal inscriptions upon it are on its south face.

[These consist of a number of cups, some surrounded by one ring, others by several, and nearly all are connected by a large number of grooves.]

"Not far from Staigue bridge, built into a fence, and close to the ruins of a stone fort, Mr. Hitchcock found a stone exhibiting two circles with some small shallow round holes. Of this stone one may say with certainty that the inscription was cut upon it when it had its present size and form. It is rounded and water-worn, and clearly not a fragment of a larger inscribed stone or rock."

Until the year 1864, very little comparatively was known to antiquaries of carved megalithic chambers, then, however, further information of a most important character suddenly reached the archæological world. In the pages of the *Meath Herald* for October 21st, 1865, appeared a letter from Mr. G. V. Du Noyer, a constant fellow worker with Mr. E. A. Conwell, of Trim, a member both of the Royal Irish Academy and of the Kilkenny Archæological Society, to whom is said to be entirely due the merit of the discoveries related ; the letter was thought of sufficient importance to be republished in the following number of the paper, in response to a warmly expressed request for the same. It said :—

"Slieve-na-Caillighe, or the Hill of the Hag or Witch, comprises the range of hills, which attain to nearly 1,000 feet in height, overlooking the demesne of Loughcrew and the plains of Clonabreany from the north, and the valley of the river Blackwater, for the distance of about six miles to the east of Oldcastle, from the south. The ridge consists of three well defined summits, the most westerly being known as Cairn Bane. These summits are occupied by groups of ancient Celtic Pagan sepulchral cairns, each containing chambers formed by large flags set on edge and rough pillar stones, principally of sandstone and calcareous grit. Originally each of these was roofed in by large slates of dry masonry, the stones overlapping each other till a rude bee-hive-formed chamber was constructed, the dome being closed in by a single flagstone. Access to these chambers was by a narrow passage, roofed with flat stones, and usually facing to the east. When the dome and passage were completed, the whole was covered up so as to form a large conical mound of broken stones, around the outer base of which rows of large flags were placed on end, thus forming a rude pyramid, visible for miles around.

"During the early part of last year the attention of Eugene Conwell, Esq., of Trim, was directed to these cairns; accordingly, at the expenditure of much private time, and of labour that a less energetic person would have shrunk from, he explored the mountain, and kindly reported to me that he had discovered a Celtic necropolis in the county of Meath. After many days spent in almost unaided researches in two of the cairns whose chambers had been exposed, Mr. Conwell succeeded in making rubbings of nineteen carved stones, and rough plans of the various groups of cairns on the three summits; with these materials in hand, he read papers on the subject before the Royal Irish Academy in May and November, 1864, parts of which were published in their 'Proceedings'; and thus the interesting discovery he had made, became generally known to the archæological world.

"With an enthusiasm that deserves all praise, Mr. Conwell, not satisfied with the partial exploration of what he then knew to be a mine of pre-historic antiquarian wealth, brought the matter prominently before the lord of the soil, James Lennox Naper, Esq., of Loughcrew; and he found no difficulty in enlisting the enlightened sentiments of that gentleman to bring to its proper conclusion the work thus happily begun, by a systematic exploration of every tumulus on the range of Slieve-na-Cailligho. Mr. Naper's agent, Charles W. Hamilton, Esq.,—a gentleman well known to science —was at once communicated with, and the work of exploration was shortly afterwards commenced. In the month of August last, Mr. Hamilton, Mr. Conwell, and myself, visited the place, and with Mr. Naper a plan of operations was decided on. In the following month Mr. Conwell undertook to inspect as many men as Mr. Naper would supply for the work, and see that the cairns were carefully opened, the contents of the central chambers cleared out, and any relics of antiquity which they might contain, secured.

"British Archæologists owe their thanks to Mr. Naper for giving such material aid to the interesting work now so admirably completed; and—I write it advisedly—the antiquarian tourist may now study a series of Celtic sepulchral remains, which in point of magnificence, number, and quaint ornamentation, surpass anything of the kind as yet discovered in Western Europe.

"In plan, the chambers are for the most part cruciform, the shaft representing the entrance passage, and the termination of the arms, the small cists, from four to five feet square, arranged around the central chamber, which in one instance (at the Chair cairn) is octagonal. Almost invariably the mouth of the passage faces from E. to E.S.E., and its position is marked by one or more large flag-stones, placed at the outer periphery of the circle, in such a way as to cut off a portion of it—a peculiarity of structure which was first noticed by Mr. Conwell.

" The strange style of ornamentation observable on many of the chambers or cists is apparently of three kinds—punched work, chiselled work, and scraped work (the first being the most common, and the last very unusual) ; and though the carved stones exceed one hundred in number, there are not two decorations alike.

" In the cists which have been long exposed to the destruction of the atmosphere, the punched or other work is much obliterated ; but in those lately opened the ornamentations are as fresh as at the hour the rude Celt departed with superstitious awe from the gloomy death chamber of his chief or king, and thanked his deity that the work was done with all honour to the mighty dead, and praise to the skilful architect and cunning sculptor.

" The ornamentation may be thus described :—Small circles, with or without a central dot ; two or many more concentric circles ; a small circle with a central dot, surrounded by a spiral line ; the single spiral ; the double spiral, or two spirals starting from differ-ent centres ; rows of small lozenges and ovals ; stars of six to thirteen rays ; wheels of nine rays ; flower ornaments, sometimes enclosed in a circle or wide oval ; wave-like lines ; groups of lunct-shaped lines ; pothooks ; small squares attached to each other side by side, so as to form a reticulated pattern ; small attached con-centric circles ; large and small hollows ; a cup hollow surrounded by one or more circles ; lozenges crossed from angle to angle (these and the squares produced by scrapings) ; an ornament like the spine of a fish with the ribs attached, or the fibre system of some leaf ; short equi-armed crosses starting sometimes from a dot and small circle ; a circle with rays round it, and the whole contained in a circle ; a series of compressed semi-circles like the letters ∩∩∩ inverted ; vertical lines far apart, with ribs sloping downwards from them like twigs ; an ornament like the fibre system of a broad leaf, with the stem attached ; rude concentric circles with short rays extending from part of the outer one; an ornament very like the simple Greek fret, with dots in the centre of the loop ; five zigzag lines, and two parallel lines, on each of which, and pointing towards each other, is a series of cones ornamented by lines radiating from the apex, crossed by others parallel to the base—this design has been produced by scraping, and I propose to call it, the Patella

ornament, as it strikingly resembles the large species of that shell
so common on our coasts, and which shell Mr. Conwell discovered
in numbers in some of the cists, in connexion with fragments of
pottery and human bones ; a semicircle with three or four straight
lines proceeding from it, but not touching it ; a dot with several
lines radiating from it; combinations of short straight lines arranged either at right angles to, or sloping from, a central line ;
an ∽ shaped curve, each loop enclosing concentric circles ; and a
vast number of other combinations of the circle, spiral, line and
dot, which cannot be described in writing.

"When decorative carving such as I have described is attempted
by any semicivilized people, as the builders of these sepulchral
cairns must have been, we naturally expect to find amongst it some
representations of objects commonly known or familiar to the
builders, as well as indications of their particular kind of worship,
—and, if they had a written language, some of its letters : with
this idea in view, I have drawn and studied all the carvings in
question ; and I think, if we allow a little play to our imagination,
without asserting anything as positive, and willing at once to admit
that mere probability is the strongest reason we can adduce for our
suppositions, that, with reference to the object of their worship, we
may regard the carving described as a circle, surrounded by short
rays and enclosed in a circle, as representing the sun ; the flower-
like ornament, also enclosed either in a circle or oval, pourtraying
the moon ; whilst the numerous dots and hollows, more or less
deep, indicated the stars ; for I should hesitate to suppose that the
figure by which we now symbolize a star was used by the rude
Celtæ of Pagan Ireland with the same signification as it had
amongst the early Christians.   To this ornament therefore, we must
attach some other meaning.

"It is remarkable that one of the groups of small hollows very
closely resembles the constellation of the Plough—the similitude
to which would be perfect if we omit one dot in the centre of what
would be the southern side of the constellation, and suppose that
the most westerly star was placed much too far to the north.

"In all rude Pagan nations we must expect that their religion
would consist of two great elements, viz., the spiritual and the
sensual ; and therefore, I was not surprised to find amongst these
carvings what may possibly be emblems of Priapian import.   With
regard to letters, I find what I believe are short Oghamic inscriptions ; and this is a point the determination of which is of the ut-
most importance, for up to the present the Ogham letter has been

regarded as early Christian, while its occurrence here proves it to be Pagan. With reference to common objects, it is possible we may have the representation of the landing of a boat, with high poop and stern, against a cliff; the water is expressed by shallow scolloped lines, and the cliff by a single line passing beneath the scollops, and rising up in front of the boat.

"Another figure is like a deep, wicker work-basket, with two slender handles, each ending in a loop ; and another figure, which consists of a series of concentric lines, forming about two thirds of the circle, and partially enclosing a small oval of two lines, would not inaptly represent an ancient wooden shield, like that preserved in the Museum of the Royal Irish Academy, the small oval being the raised conical boss, while the concentric lines were the alternate concentric ridges and grooves with which the shield is ornamented.

" Another group of lunet-shaped lines might well be supposed to represent one of those gold torque or collar-like ornaments which are also in the Museum of the Academy. Another figure might be likened to a two-wheeled chariot, with a semi-circular hood over it.

" I cannot detect the form of anything like a weapon, unless we suppose those small diamond patterns represent spears and arrow heads.

" With regard to the objects of high antiquarian interest which Mr. Conwell found during the course of his excavations, I shall leave them to him to describe—my object in putting together these remarks being a simple explanation of a most remarkable class of Celtic remains, the events which led to their discovery and exploration, and the part which I was fortunately enabled to take in the work.

" It is worthy of remark that some of the ancient British carvings on natural rock surfaces in Northumberland and the Eastern borders are precisely similar to some of those discovered at Slicena-Caillighe ; for example, the dot and circle, the incomplete concentric oval, the horse-shoe ornament, the simple dot, the ∩ shaped character, and several others."

In the summer of the year 1864, Mr. George Du Noyer, Geologist, while making an examination of the district east of Oldcastle, in the county of Meath, discovered some examples of carving on a natural rock surface, which he described as unique in the East of Ireland, so far as information then went. They were found on the glacialized surface of an inclined bed of lower Silurian grit, near the summit of Ryefield Hill, in the townland of Ballydorragh, county Cavan, one mile and a half to the north of the Virginia Road station, on the Meath railway.

"The marking are all produced by simple scraping with a saw-like motion; and some of them, if not all, must have been formed by a metal instrument. The figures most commonly represented are detached straight-armed crosses; but not unfrequently these are so grouped or clustered together as to form a network of lines crossing in every direction; in two instances these crosses are inclosed in four lines, or rather an oblong rectangular figure is crossed from angle to angle; sometimes a single line is crossed by two smaller lines near each other, and again one arm of the cross is terminated by a short blunt line, or an arrow headed depression; all these markings, from the mode of their construction, are deeper at the central portion of the lines than at the extremities, which fine off.

" Some of the crosses had a fresh look, as if but recently scraped; but the majority of them were either partially or totally concealed by a thick coating of lichen, the growth of many centuries, and they had to be carefully cleaned before their forms could be determined."

Besides the scrapings thus described other markings were found, evidently produced by chiselling, and quite sharp in their outlines. All the information which the geologist was able to obtain in the neighbourhood was that they were the work of fairies on state nights, such as St. John's Eve. Mr. Du Noyer ventured to suggest that the children who used this stone as a playground, might have made these crosses for their amusement; this, however, was at once repudiated, though it was admitted the stone was often used as a slide by the young people who frequented the locality.

Two years after making the above discovery, Mr. Du Noyer was again "fortunate enough," to use his own words, to discover some other remarkable markings produced by scraping and punching on a natural rock surface, 350 yards N.N.E. of Calliagh Dirra's House, Townland of Paddock, Co. Louth.

These markings are in many respects similar to those on the rocks of Cavan, already described, but they differ in some particulars, some of them being of quite a Runic character, and from their being covered with a thick coating of lichen, evidently of the remotest antiquity. Two of these devices are described as resembling the Roman letters P I, yet this resemblance is in Mr. Du

Noyer's opinion accidental ; just as some of the devices from the megalithic chambers of Slieno-na-Callighe, and also some of the carved rocks in Sweden, closely resemble a pair of spectacles, though no one for a moment could think that they had such a significance.

Mr. Noyer describes the most remarkable of the devices on this rock as a cross of eight arms, resting on a short flat pedestal. ' If this latter feature were removed, we have a close resemblance to the Runic letter H ; the mark which resembles the letter P is very similar to the rune of the same significance ; and the small simple cross, the upright arm being the longer, is quite like the Runic letter E.'

In the *Dublin Examiner* for October, 1816, we find a short account of some Irish inscribed stones from the pen of Dr. Petrie. After complaining of the general neglect of the study of Irish Antiquities, he says :—" We have been induced to prefix the preceding observations to this short article on Irish Antiquities, in the hope of drawing the attention of some of our readers to such pursuits.

" The inscribed stones on the accompanying plate, are all in the county of Dublin, and have been hitherto unnoticed. No. 1 appears to represent the sun and moon, the principal deities of the pagan Irish. It is a rude stone of mountain granite deeply inscribed, and, together with another of nearly the same size, uninscribed, and a stone seat or chair, constitute the remains of an ancient temple near the village of Killina. This temple, not very many years since, contained two other chairs, similar to the one remaining, one of which we have seen in an adjoining field ; and was encompassed by a circle of stones, eighteen or twenty in number. These stones have either been removed, or are covered with an embankment, which appears to have been thrown up around it. The area within the circle has been converted to a kitchen garden, and when first turned up, some ornaments, celts and spear heads, were, we understand, discovered. About twenty-five or thirty years ago, a number of rude slate coffins, containing skeletons, were found between the temple and shore, and about ten years since, five large urns of backed clay, containing calcined bones, were dug up in the village of Killina.

" This temple is curious to the antiquary, from the peculiarity of its containing seats, which, if judges' (Brehon's) chairs, as called traditionally by the people, corroborates the opinion that has been given in a celebrated periodical work, that the circles remaining in

Great Britain and Ireland, were temples where law was adminis-
tered. Yet, on the other hand, the inscription seems to indicate
that it was dedicated to religious rites, or, at least, that such were
blended with the judicial ceremonies of those remote times.

" No. 2 is a chiselled stone of mountain granite in the churchyard
of Rathmichael, at Shankhill, near Loughlin's town ; it is broken
in the middle, and is employed as two head-stones. The inscription
is deep and perfect. There are two or three other stones similarly
inscribed, but less perfectly preserved ; and it may be remarked
that they are the only ones of the granite kind to be met there,
the building, as well as the mountain on which it stands, being of
another description ; from which it may be inferred that they were
brought, perhaps, from a considerable distance, for the purpose to
which they are now converted. Of the meaning of the symbol
which is inscribed on these stones, we are diffident of hazarding a
conjecture. We shall, however, mention that we have read some-
where, that the ancient Irish represented the Ti-mor, or Great God,
by a circle, and also by concentric circles, and volutes ; and that
it was the opinion of a celebrated antiquary (General Vallancey),
now deceased, with whom we have conversed on this subject, that
such was the signification of such symbols.

" No. 3 is a symbol of the same kind in the churchyard of Croagh,
about two miles beyond Rathfarnham."

Dean Graves, commenting upon this, says :—" Dr. Petrie would
now speak with less deference to the authority of General Vallancey ; and I am much mistaken if he would not refer these monuments, which appear to be artificially squared, to the early Christian period. If I am right in assuming that they do not belong to
the Pagan time, and that they were sepulchral stones, we shall be
warranted in concluding that whatever these symbols represent,
there was an appropriateness in inscribing them on monuments of
a sepulchral kind."

The attention of the Rev. James Graves was called some years
ago to a very fine pillar stone at Muff, about five miles from Londonderry, and in 1872, when he examined and sketched the same,
he found that one of its faces was covered with cup and circle
sculpturings, some of which had the central channels which appear
on the rock sculptures in Kerry—there were as many as fifteen
cups, all of them surrounded by shallow rings. In the autumn of
1874, the ground round the base of this stone was carefully excavated by several well-known antiquarians ; it was then found to
measure eight feet in height, its broadest face was four feet six

inches across, diminishing to three feet six inches on the opposite face, the sides being as nearly as possible two feet six inches wide. The broadest side was wonderfully plain and smooth, but quite unsculptured ; the angles much worn and smooth as if by the rubbing of cattle. The carving was all on the lesser face, looking S.E., or towards Londonderry ; and the peasantry say that the cup markings are the indentations of cannon balls which struck it at the time of the famous siege. Where the soil had covered the base, two of the cups with their concentric circles were very plain and unworn ; but the water trickling from a hollow on the top of the stone had injured some of those above. Excavations were made to a depth of four feet round the base of the menhir ; but no trace of interment, or relic of any kind was discovered. Close to the stone was found a kind of bone earth, or soil mixed with minute fragments of bone, apparently not human, but from their minute and decomposed state indentification was impossible.*

Mr. Graves, in allusion to the above, says :—" Although the cup and circle are thus found in Ireland, apparently used both on Pagan and Christian monuments, excepting this pillar stone at Muff, I know of no other instance in Ireland, besides those described by Bishop Graves, which exhibits the channel proceeding from the central cup. That these sculptures had a meaning cannot be denied, but it seems yet undiscovered. Bishop Graves's reasons against their having anything to do with early ideas of astronomy, are unanswerable ; but I fear his explanation of these sculptures as being maps of the relative position of the circular earth-works or raths on the face of the country will not be accepted as conclusive. It does not appear that in the parts of Scotland and northern England where these rock-sculptures occur most numerously, there are many raths, if any at all occur ; whilst in Ireland, which abounds with these earth-works, rock-sculptures of this class, at least as observed, are extremely rare. The age of the cup and circle marks seems also, still undecided."

" If it were the case that these sculpturings, which all seemed to have been picked, not scribed or rubbed, could be effected only by metal tools, it would, so far, give some support to Bishop Graves's idea, viz., that they were contemporary with the raths—nay, posterior in date to some of these structures, which cannot in any case be relegated to the stone age ; but Mr. Daniel Wilson, in his notice of some cup markings, observed by him in Ohio and Kentucky,

* Kilkenny Arch. Jour., 1877.

U.S., gives it as his opinion that they could be formed by flint implements, inclining, however, to the idea that, in many cases, they were formed by rubbing. That some cup hollows on flat rocks may be formed by the solvent property of rain water is undoubted ; but when the groupings of the cups shows design, or where they are surrounded by circles, and have channels issuing from them, this latter explanation of their formation must be put aside." *

In the year 1886, Mr. W. F. Wakeman of the Kilkenny Archæological Association wrote that he was happy to announce the finding on the Ponsonby Estate, in the neighbourhood of Youghal, of a truly magnificent and characteristic example of the mysterious class of engravings known as cup and ring marks. He said :— " Just before the conclusion of our recent meeting, held in Waterford, through the interest of the Rev. James Graves the monument in question became the property of our Association. It may now be seen in the museum at Kilkenny, where it forms an object of striking interest. The stone, which was found with some others, does not appear to have formed part of any building. I understand that it lay nearly buried in the soil. The other stones were said to be unmarked by a tool, and may, or may not, have been intended as memorials. The material is extremely hard whinstone, of a silvery grey colour when fractured. Of the scribings which it bears, the principal consists of nine concentric circles, deeply cut, enclosing a cup-hollow, from which extends the characteristic channel. The latter stretches slightly beyond the outermost circle. There are altogether about twenty-six cups of different sizes. Of these, the largest, which is somewhat oval in form, is very remarkable in having round its edges a raised ridge. Besides the ordinary cup-hollows are four oblong depressions, which, doubtlessly, owe their peculiarity of form to some intention, the drift of which it would, with our present amount of information on such subjects, be impossible to determine."

Outside the chamber of Knockmany, county Tyrone, Ireland, are three blocks of old red sandstone, which are believed to have formed the roof of the chamber, of which, says Mr. Wakeman, "no other relics are at present visible. The enclosure is in shape an oblong, measuring internally ten feet three, by six feet six inches. Two of the blocks have fallen inwardly, and lie on their faces, so that without considerable labour it is impossible to deter-

* Kilkenny Arch. Journl., 1877.

mine whether they present scorings or otherwise. A third stone stands near the north western angle (measuring about four feet six inches in height, by three feet two inches in breadth) upon which are carved a number of mystic symbols, such as we find on the stones within the chambers of New Grange, Dowth, and Slievenacalliagh. Some of the work has a very oghamic look, but in no instance here are the strokes returned on the sides of the leac."

On this stone we have groups of six and seven rings surrounding a depressed centre, also parallel, curved and angular markings.

There is a third stone, four feet eight inches in height, by two feet ten inches in breadth. 'It is ten inches and a half in thickness, and on this narrow surface, on the interior have been carved most singular designs. These consist of groups of horizontal scorings very well marked, three deeply indented cups, and some lines which seem to have formed portion of a compound semicircle. All the other upright stones would seem to have been anciently untouched by a graver, but in not a few spots they bear modern names and dates, which have been wantonly carved or scratched by visitors who ambitioned to see themselves thus recorded. Unfortunately, the hill is a favourite site for picnic parties from Clogher, Omagh, and neighbouring districts.'

"The strokes on the above stones," Mr. Wakeman says, he need not say, " are not to be classed with any recognised or acknowledged Ogham letters hitherto described. Nevertheless, it can scarcely be doubted that they were intended, along with their neighbouring carvings, to convey some meaning. It would be simply absurd to attribute to them an alphabetic character. They are probably signs or symbols which were well understood at the date of their execution. One cannot help wishing that a time may arrive when these and like scorings would lose much of the mystery in which they are at present shrouded ; but the key appears to be lost for ever."

In October, 1888, Mr. G. Kinahan, of Donegal, described the stones and antiquities of the Mevagh hamlet, near the north-west shore of Mulroy Bay, county Donegal. He mentioned a long crag formed by a massive felstone dyke found a little south of the hamlet, and on the surface of this, about sixty feet long, and of width varying from fifteen to twenty-five feet, "are numerous inscriptions, generally more or less in groups, while others are scattered about separately. Indeed, in other places on the crag, single inscriptions were detected, but so indistinct and isolated that they attracted little notice." The rock surfaces, he says, were very much weathered, and in places were clothed with a thin peat; some of the markings on the flat top surface of the crag were so far effaced that no attempt was made to copy them, rubbings were taken, however, of the best preserved and most prominent groups. "From these it was seen that the scribings in general consisted of combinations of circles, cups, and furrows, sometimes a cup being surrounded by circles, but often the former having a channel leading from it. In some, however, the cup was replaced by a ball. Occasionally the circles were combined with a cross; in one place a cross was combined with cups; in a few places there were other forms.

"The largest and best preserved group was on a surface sloping about south-east. Below a peculiar and unique scribing was an elaborate combination of circles, &c. To the westward were remarkable crosses in circles."

In the locality northward of Kilmacrenan, and about half a mile east of the south end of Barnesby, occur what are called the Barnes "Dallans," or Standing Stones. "The largest of the Dallans is a massive flagstone, seven feet high above the ground, and seven feet wide; the smaller one (there are two of them) which is six feet high, by five feet in the widest part, seems to have been worked to represent the head of a huge spear."

"On the western face of the large dallan there is one cup, and a faintly marked cross. On the eastern face there is a very elaborate sculpturing, down to a foot and a half below the present surface, and at the lower south-east margin there is a curious combination of circles, furrows and cups. The upper portion of the northern side of the eastern face, has markings, if possible, even still more remarkable. This conspicuous group consists of cup and saucer designs, connected by furrows, the whole effect giving an appearance as if they were a spray of æsthetic flowers. Seven cups are here found in a nearly horizontal line, which may have some meaning, as also a circle of cups round a cup and saucer to the south.

"Scribed stones are not uncommon in the eastern, or rather north-eastern, portion of the county Donegal, but in general they consist solely of cup-markings."

In Lewis's Topographical Dictionary, vol. 2, p. 669, occurs the following:—"In the parish of Errigalkerago is a flat stone, set upright, about three feet broad, and of the same height above ground, having one side covered with carvings of a regular design, consisting of waving and circular lines ; it had been the covering of a vault formed of flags set edge-way. In the vault were found two earthen vessels containing ashes."

Mr. Kinahan concludes his paper thus :--"The Donegal cup-markings are sometimes numerous, but usually there are only seven, called 'giant's finger-marks,' as they are said to be the impression of his fingers when pushing the stone, which is often called a ' giant's finger-stone.' The cup marks are found on natural rock surfaces—as on the summit of Culbrue and the hill south-west of Lough Salt ; on erratics, as at Trintagh and elsewhere ; on ' standing-stones,' as on the hill near Litter ; on ' cover-stones ' of cromlechs, as at Goldrum ; and on flat stones in ancient structures. Roughly-rounded stones on which more or less cup-marks occur, are—numerous cups on the stone called ' St. Columbkill's Bed,' in the parish of Gartan, and west of Lough Akibbon ; in the same parish, very many on a stone at the side of the road from Church-hill to Glendowan ; and on a stone in the old deer-park of Castle-forward. The last was described, at the beginning of the century, by Dr. McParlan, in his ' Statistical History,' as standing on uprights. It is now dismantled, broken in two, and one half carried away.

" The Mevagh scribings, although not so elaborate in design, yet resemble in a slight degree those in the tombs of the De Danaan at Lough Crew, and also those in the sculptured caves of the Fermanagh Hills. The cup and saucer designs of the Barnes dallans are somewhat allied, but more elaborate, to the so-called ' St. Patrick's Knee marks,' on ' St. Patrick's Chair,' south-west of Westport, where he used to pray on his way to Croaghpatric."

Sligo, Ireland, has a number of rude stone monuments whose markings are of a character, for the most part, altogether different from the ordinary cups and rings found in other districts. This is particularly so on the lands of Cloverhill, situate about 200 yards due east of Laghtareal Hill. Here, we are told by Mr. W. G. Wood-Martin, Secretary of the Royal Historical and Archæological Association of Ireland, there are carvings of peculiar character on the interior surface of the slabs forming a cist ; and this when first stripped by the plough, about the year 1830, was entirely flagged on the bottom, or floor—in that respect differing from another smaller cist immediately adjoining, which presents only an earthen surface. The Cloverhill chamber, 5 feet 9 inches long by 3 feet 6 inches broad, now consists of nine stones, for it is not thought that one situated to the south of the entrance had originally formed part of the structure. "One of the stones has two sets of scorings—the one upon its edge, the other upon its interior surface. The markings upon its edge consist of small cup-like dots, each enclosed in a circle, also two horizontal lines thus resembling the scorings on a remarkable pillar-stone at Muff, county Derry."

The carving upon its interior surface is very singular—a number of acute angles like the letter A with the ends of the two limbs considerably curled, and some other triangular forms with the sides somewhat curved.

Other stones are marked with elaborate spirals of a style which antiquaries refer to the bronze age.

Mr. Wood-Martin says :—"These archaic markings, whether on cliffs, on simple earth, fast-rocks, or on rude stone sepulchral monuments, may probably have been the outcome of some primitive symbolical or mystical ideas of the savage mind, and thus was perpetuated on the most durable materials to hand, the meaning sought to be conveyed, until the custom became characteristic of an early class of interment. Its meaning or original symbolism, now buried in oblivion, may, perhaps, be ultimately unravelled by means of careful research, comparison, and analysis of these primitive scribings."

The island of Achill has some stones of a somewhat special character which are thus referred to in the Kilkenny Archæological Journal, for July, 1888 :—"The next monument is one of a group situated also on the slope of the mountain, and marked on the Ordnance Sheet as tumulus, cromlech, Danish ditch, etc., respectively. The blocks of stone that remain had evidently formed the supports of the ancient covering-slab, which has now disappeared. The cup-markings on the largest of the remaining supports presents a peculiar feature, these marks being rare on cromlechs or dolmens, although not uncommon on stones forming portion of mound-covered sepulchral chambers, like those of Newgrange, Dowth, Sliabh-na-caillighe, Knockmany, etc. On a structure of the Cromlech, or uncovered class of monuments, cup-markings have not been elsewhere found in Ireland, except in rare instances —as, for example, the one at Clochtogle, near Lisbellaw, county Fermanagh. In both instances the cup markings are equal in number, and diminish in size as they extend from left to right; this arrangement clearly indicates intention, and the strong likeness existing between work upon sepulchral structures so widely separated is worthy of note."

Although rock markings all over the world have certain features in common, those of some nations are so perfectly characteristic and distinct from those of others that there will be no fear of their being confounded. The inscriptions found in the great mounds of New Grange and Dowth, on the Boyne, are very different from those of the North of England and Scotland. "One of the chief characteristics of the latter is that most of the circular incised figures are concentric with a central cup-like hollow, and a channel passing through the concentric arches; while those at New Grange and Dowth are as a rule spirals, without the central hollow or intersecting channel, and are associated with fern-leaf patterns, and also with lozenge, zigzag and chevron-like markings, which are analogous to the ornamentation of the fictile sepulchral vessels occurring in these islands, generally supposed to be Celtic, and the massive penannular rings and flat lunulæ of fine gold, so many examples of which have been found in Ireland."

Those who have an opportunity of consulting Sir William Wilde's Beauties of the Boyne (said to be the best and fullest account extant) will find a number of plates which give a most excellent idea of the character of these particular cuttings. Sir William writes:— "When we first visited New Grange, some twelve years ago, the entrance was greatly obscured by brambles, and a heap of loose stones which had ravelled out from the adjoining mound. This entrance which is nearly square, and formed by large flags, the continuation of the stone passage already alluded to, is now at a considerable distance from the original outer circle of the mound, and consequently the passage is at present much shorter than it was originally, if, indeed, it ever extended so far as the outer circle. A few years ago, a gentleman, then residing in the neighbourhood, cleared away the stones and rubbish which obscured the mouth of the cave, and brought to light a very remarkably carved stone, which now slopes from the entrance. This we thought at the time was quite a discovery, inasmuch as none of the modern writers had noticed it. The Welsh antiquary, however, thus describes it :— 'The entry into this cave is at bottom, and before it we found a great flat stone, like a large tombstone, placed edgeways, having on the outside certain barbarous carvings like snakes encircled, but without heads.'

"This stone, so beautifully carved in spirals and volutes, is slightly convex, from above downwards; it measures ten feet in length, and is about eighteen inches thick. What its original use was,—where its original position in this mound—whether its carvings exhibit the same handiwork and design as those sculptured stones in the interior, and whether this beautiful slab did not belong to some other building of anterior date—are questions worthy of consideration."

Mr. Graves says :—" The most singular thing about these carvings, is, that they seem in some instances at least, not to have been originally made for the purpose of ornamenting the great sepulchral structure in which they are now found, as is proved by the occurrence of the markings on the surfaces of the stones now concealed from view, and this in portions where it would be impossible to carve them after the erection of the structure."

We turn again to the " Beauties of the Boyne," and find the following, which Mr. Graves calls a corroboration of his own experience. " The following very remarkable circumstance struck us while investigating this ancient structure of New Grange. We found that those carvings not only covered portions of the stones exposed to view, but extended over those surfaces which, until some recent delapidation, were completely concealed from view, and where a tool could not have reached them ; and the inference is plain, that these stones were carved prior to their being placed in their present position ; perhaps were used for some anterior purpose. If so, how much it adds to their antiquity. The eastern jamb of the chamber, opposite the entrance, has fallen in wards, and recently exposed a portion of the under surface of a great flag, which is now, for the first time since the erection of the building, exposed to view. This flag has, like most of the other stones here, a sort of skin, or brownish outer polish, as if water-washed. Now, in all the exposed carvings upon the other stones, the indentures have assumed more or less of the dark colour and polish around ; whereas in this one the colour of the cutting and the track of the tool is just as fresh as if done but yesterday."

Sir William Wilde then proceeds to describe the interior of the cave or chamber of New Grange, in which there are several apartments of various sizes more or less enriched with rude carvings, volutes, lozenges, zigzags, and spiral lines, cut into the stones, and in some instances standing out in relief.

Upon a careful examination of the spiral carvings he found them nearly all formed of a double coil, commencing with a loop, and in most instances, having seven turns.

The same explorer also describes the examination of certain caves at Dowth, in which were a number of blocks of stone fully as large as those found at New Grange, and several of them similarly carved. Many of the Dowth carvings, however, which present great beauty of design, differ somewhat from those at New Grange. " We find here," he says, " in addition to those already figured, a number of wheel-like ornaments and concentric circles, and others with lines radiating from a point ; while some very much resemble the Ogham character, consisting of short, straight, parallel lines. In some instances we find the representation of a lotus, or lily-leaf, carved with such precision as to give it at first view the appearance of a fossil. And what adds to the interest of these sculptures, is, that the leaf stands out about half an inch in relief, while all the surrounding stone, for many feet adjoining, has been picked away with infinite care and labour."

CHAPTER V.

Rock markings in Scotland.

ON Jan. 4th, 1882, a communication was made to the British Archæological Association, by Mr. J. T. Irvine, of Lichfield, respecting cup-markings found in Scotland. He said :—"With regard to the stones presenting cup-shaped sinkings which are found in Scotland, in certain places around the coasts of the Shetland Islands, sinkings of a similar description are found. These are found, it has been said by a good local authority, at points where in general a boat could run into and land a person on the rock at certain times of the tide. Those I have seen were in each case more than one in number, and irregularly placed : speaking from memory, about, it might be, 2 to 2½ inches deep, and wide enough to turn round three fingers in. Instances are found at Funzie or Finyie, in Fetlar and in Yell, on the north side of the Voes of Snarravoe, and at or below Palyabag, Clivocast, Uyuasound. A singular notice of certain cup-marks which I have not myself seen, is found in the account of the Scattald Marches of the Island of Unst, a transcript of which is here added :—

"'Skā Scattald, being Outer and Hamer Skā begins with Norwick at the North Sea, at a knowe in the middle of Liddadaal, thence with Norwick, Scattald on the right hand, southward, up to Sodersfail, where is a stone standing endlong, with three holes in it, the middle hole whereof is broke out, to a great grey stone, near which stands a stone endlong, with a small stone set upright to the top of it ; and thence, with Norwick still on the right, stretching to a great heap of stones or ancient building, called Housen-vard, and from thence to Clifts of Skā and Norwick to a place called the Catthouse, right beneath which, at the foot of the banks is a solid rock into which three holes, near each other, are artificially made, which is the southmost sea march separating Skā from Norwick."

Mr. Lawson Tait, Surgeon, Golspie, supplies a note of a Kist with a cup-marked cover, found in a mound on the Links of Dornoch. He says :—"On the 12th of April, 1867, I opened a large tumulus situated on the Dornoch Links, about a mile to the east of the town, and about 500 yards from the shore. It was 11 feet in height, and nearly 30 feet in diameter. It was composed of rubble work and earth. After removing about three feet of stones and earth from the surface, I exposed a large flag of yellow sandstone, 6 ft. 4 inches long, by 4 ft. 10 inches broad. On it were various cup-shaped markings. They are distinctly artificial in appearance, every one, even the very smallest, bearing the rugged impression of a rude tool. I have produced very similar cup-markings by chipping flint flakes with an iron tool upon a flat sandstone. On raising a flag a kist was exposed, which contained a few shreds of bones, lying apparently in position, and one tolerably well finished flint-head. The dimensions of the kist were 3 feet 7 inches long, 2 feet 4 inches wide, and 2 feet 1 inch deep. Its long measurement was north-west and south-east. The sides were formed of large sandstone slabs set on end, and there was a floor formed of smaller flags. There was no indication of the position of the body."

In the year 1785, a drawing was presented to the Royal Society of Edinburgh, by Colonel Hugh Montgomery, of Shielmorly, of an incised slab which had formed the cover of a cist at Coilsfield in Ayrshire, and in which was an urn filled with incinerated bones. The cist was discovered in digging a gravel pit, and a picture of the cover may be seen in Wilson's ' Prehistoric Annals of Scotland ' (vol. 1, p. 480). The principal figure on it is the same as our common typical form ; six concentric circles around a cup from which issues a groove ; but along with this is a coiled or spiral figure, of which, says Mr. Tait, we have no example in Northumberland. The dimensions of the stone were about five feet in length, by two feet six inches in breadth.

Dr. Wilson says:—"The site of this rudely sculptured cist is associated by popular tradition with the legendary eponymus of the district ; and a later discovery of cinerary urns at the same spot has been assumed to authenticate one of the many apocryphal records which history professes to have chronicled regarding him. Near Coilsfield house is a large tumulus, crowned with two huge blocks of granite, which local tradition affirmed to mark the place of sepulture of the redoubted hero, of whom Boece records :—" King Coyll, unwarly kepit be his nobiles, was slane, in memory whereof the place quhare he was slane was namit efter Coyll; quhilk regioun remains yit under the same name or litill different thairfra, callit now Kyle." Certain zealous local antiquaries having resolved to put tradition to the test, the tumulus was opened in 1837, and found to enclose a cist covered by a circular stone about three feet in diameter, beneath which four plain urns were disposed, the largest of which measured nearly eight inches in height. The author of a recent topographical work on the district of Kyle gravely assumes this discovery as giving to the traditionary evidence, and to the statements of early Scottish historians, in regard to Coil, except with respect to the date, a degree of probability higher than they formerly possessed. What more might not the antiquaries of Kyle have been able to establish had they known of the older discovery on the same spot, and of the mysterious symbols traced on the sepulchral stone."

In Loch-an-Haalkal in Scotland, is an island with a castle on it, said to have been built by Hacon for a hunting seat; the walls are an irregular square, 6 or 7 feet thick, and 5 or 6 feet high, built without mortar, and with flat stones, the same as the Pictish towers, It is said that a causeway ran from the island to the mainland, a distance of 20 or 30 yards ; the water is now, however, 6 or 7 feet deep. On the edge of the precipitous bank of the loch, and exactly opposite the island, there is a large boulder with a flat top, and on this there are a number of cups and rings. The people say they were made by the high heels of a fairy who lived in the castle. This stone is not generally known. The gamekeeper who first shewed it to Mr. Horsburgh of Lochmalony, from whom, we get the above, thought it was for playing some game.

At Lochgilphead in Argyleshire is a stone both holed and cup-marked. It has been figured in the " Sculptured Stones of Scotland," but no description of it is there given. A full account of these holed stones may be seen in two other volumes issued by the publisher of this work, one entitled " Phallicism," and the other, " Phallic Objects, Monuments and Remains." It is there explained that oaths were taken and contracts ratified by passing the hands through these openings, while, in other cases, where the hole was larger, the entire body was passed through as representative of the new birth. " It is quite certain," remarks the author of the " Rude Stone Monuments," " that the oath to Woden or Odin was sworn by persons joining hands through the hole in this ring stone, and that an oath so taken, although by Christians, was deemed solemn and binding. This ceremony was held so very sacred in those times, that the person who dared to break the engagement made there was accounted infamous and excluded from society. Principal Gordon, in his " Journey to the Orkney Islands," in 1781, relates the following anecdote :—" The young man was called before the session, and the elders were particularly severe. Being asked by the minister the cause of so much severity, they answered,

'You do not know what a bad man this is; he has broken the promise of Odin,' and further explained that the contracting parties had joined hands through the hole in the stone."

The stone at Lochgilphead, which is remarkable for the reason above mentioned, has a hole at the lower part, and some fifteen cups above it.

A rough but elaborately engraved slab known as the "Annan Street Stone," was discovered some years ago upon the farm of Wheathope, at a place called Annan Street, a drawing of which was made by George Scott, the friend of Mungo Park, the traveller. The drawing was sent by Sir Walter Scott to the Society of Antiquaries of Scotland in 1828, who described the original as a rough sandstone, about six feet long by two and a half broad ; it was marked "a Druid stone found at Annan Street, figured with the sun and moon." Dr. Wilson says little doubt can be entertained that it had formed the cover of a cist, though few probably will now be inclined to attempt a solution of the enigmatic devices rudely traced on its surface. The spot where it was found is about half a mile from the church at Yarrow, and close by there are two monoliths about 120 yards apart, which popular tradition associates with the combat that has given "The dowie houms of Yarrow," so touching a place in the legendary poetry of Scotland. Thus does the human mind delight to give a local habitation to the mythic and traditional characters and incidents that take hold of the fancy, whether it be the old mythological smith Wayland, associated with the cromlech of Berkshire ; the fabulous king Coil, and the sepulchral barrow of Ayrshire ; or the Flower of Yarrow, the creation of some nameless Scottish minstrel, whose pathetic ballad will live as long as our language endures.

The rude attempts at sculpture figured here are certainly as artless, and to us as meaningless, as the chance traces of wind and tide on the deserted sea-beach. Doubtless they had a meaning and an object once, and, were not produced without the expenditure both of time and labour by the primitive artist, possibly still unprovided with metallic tools. To us they are simply of value as indicating the most infantile efforts of the old British sculptor, and the rudiments of the art which was destined to produce in later ages such gorgeous piles as the cathedral of Salisbury, and sculptures like those of Wells and York. The parent delights to trace in the prattle of his child the promise of future years ; and the archæologist may be pardoned if tempted at times to linger too fondly on such infantile efforts, in which he recognises the germs of

E

future arts, the first attempts at symbolic prefigurements and rudiments of those representative signs from which have sprung letters and all that followed in their train."

The markings on this Annan Stone are in many respects similar to others, but they appear to have certain variations which are not altogether as common. Some are parallel zigzags, some parallel double curves, others are concentric rings, while others again are spiral rings, and some, parallel straight lines.

Some thirty years ago, Mr. George Petrie, a member of the Society of Antiquaries of Scotland, supplied us with some interesting particulars relative to discoveries at Pickaquay, near Kirkwall, in Orkney, and which show us how far north in the British Isles cup and ring marks occur. He had been visiting the Pict's house in the Holm of Pupa Westray opened by Lieut. Thomas, R.N., in 1849. In his description of the building that gentleman mentioned that "on the side wall near the entrance, and about 6 feet from the floor, there was a neatly engraved circle about 4 inches in diameter; there was also another stone with the appearance of having two small circles touching each other engraved upon it, but," he remarked, "it was so common to find geometrical figures upon the Orkney flags, from a semi-crystalization of the pyrites which they contain, that he was unable to decide whether those seen in the Pict's house were natural or not." Mr. Petrie says he carefully examined the walls of the main chamber at each end, and was agreeably surprised not only to find the circles referred to by Lieut. Thomas, but also to discover quite close to them, as well as on various other stones in the walls, other engraved figures. One set was on a large lintel over the entrance of the passage between the south chamber and the small cell on its east side. It was easy to see that the figures were formed by a pointed instrument tolerably sharp.

"Mr. Farrer opened a tumulus at Pickaquoy, near Kirkwall, in 1853, but this," says Mr. Petrie, "I did not see till some time afterwards, when it was in so dilapidated a state that I could not make out whether it had been a barrow containing two built cists or graves, or a Pict's house; but most probably it had been the latter. The two cells or graves were separated by a mass of building about four feet thick, and the largest, which was 8 feet long by 4 feet 6 inches wide, was to the south of the smaller one, which measured 6 feet 4 inches in length, and 4 feet in breadth, and was divided lengthways into two equal compartments by stones set on edge. The length of the cells was in the direction of east and west. About 1 foot 9 inches distant from the west end of the north wall of the largest cell a stone, with concentric circles engraved on it, was built upright in the wall. Another long slab was found with 13 small cavities along one of its edges, and a rather large cavity about the centre of one of its sides. When a short time afterwards I examined the engraved circles, and especially the cavities cut in the stones in the walls of the Pict's house at Papa Westray, the similarity was so striking, that it required no great stretch of imagination to suppose that the same instrument chiselled the figures in both places. The general appearance of the place was that of an immense grave of double the ordinary dimensions, but divided into three compartments by large upright flags or stones, whose tops were above the surface of the mound. The sides of the grave were formed by stones built in the shape of rude walls, but how much of these may have been removed before we examined the place we could not even conjecture, as the whole mound was more or less covered with loose stones." *

* Soc. Antiq. Scot. Pro., 2, p. 61.

CHAPTER VI.

Rock Markings in Sweden and Switzerland.

MR. GEORGE TATE leans somewhat to the opinion that inscriptions of the same character as ours are not to be found outside the British Islands. In Brittany, he says, where we might expect to find similar remains, there are a great many enormous standing stones ranged in eleven rows, and extending a distance of five furlongs. " Fanciful antiquarians have called this a Dracontia or Serpent Temple. On a cromlech connected with these monoliths, there are spiral and zigzag sculptures resembling those of New Grange ; but these I consider ornamental, and not symbolical. Careful researches among these wonderful megaliths, by Mr. Samuel Ferguson and M. Réné Galles have brought to light another class of sculptures which appear to possess some significance ; the forms are extraordinary, and in the general aspect of some of them, there is a resemblance to those on the perpendicular face of Cuddy's Cove in Northumberland. One is similar to the form of the mediæval M ; there is a U like character ; forms like hatchets with handles, and one the rude outline of a horned quadruped. But while having analogies to the Cuddy's Cove figures, none of them belong to the same group as the typical concentric circles of Northumberland. Mr. Ferguson regards them, however, as of great antiquity. 'The singular taste,' he says, 'and the barbaric aspect of the objects, appear to the writer to refer them to a race having more of the characteristics of the Indian and Polynesian off-shoots from the parent seats, than of any of the existing nationalities of Europe."

Somewhat more analogous to the Northumbrian symbols are some sculptures on rock temples of pre-historic age in the island of Malta. Some of these forms are rudely spiral, starting from a central boss ; others are oval, representing it is thought, the egg and serpent, emblems in Phœnician worship. I have examined the Egyptian, Assyrian, and other eastern inscriptions in the British Museum and elsewhere. but I have not been able to detect any figure like the typical forms of the Northumberland inscriptions. Circles with a central boss may be seen ; among Egyptian hieroglyphics there is a circle around a central dot ; and the same kind of circle with the addition of a short curve from the circumference, expressive of the God Phre; but nowhere is seen the circle around the hollow along with the radial groove.

One of the symbols on the Scottish stones—that which is called the spectacle ornament, formed by two groups of concentric circles around a hollow, the groups being united by two or more curved grooves—has a resemblance to some of the compound figures of Northumbrian stones; but still, the Scottish symbol has not the radial groove. The Scottish symbolical stones belong, I believe, to a later period than the Northumberland sculptures—to the age immediately preceding the introduction of Christianity.

These peculiar rock carvings which are found to such an extent scattered throughout various parts of the British Isles and America, are found also in large numbers amongst the boulders of Sweden. A work of considerable interest was published at Stockholm in 1848, by Axel Em. Holmberg, entitled the "Skandinaviens Hall-ristningar," which, both by descriptive letter-press and numerous plates, conveys a very correct idea of these local inscriptions, and some of them will be found particularly remarkable from their very great resemblance to inscribed stones in other parts of the world. This is particularly the case, as has been pointed out by Mr. J. R. Allen of the British Archæological Association, with a large block of gritstone standing on the edge of the cliff at the northern boundary of Addingham high moor, about a mile to the west of the Panorama Rock, and overhanging the valley of the Wharfe. The stone is 19 ft. long, by 7 ft. broad, by 4 ft. 6 in. thick. At the east end of it are two rock basins 1 ft. 3 in. across, and on the other is carved a most unusual device, consisting of four curved arms starting from a common centre, not altogether unlike the sails of a windmill. Strangely enough an exact counterpart of this Yorkshire stone is found at Tossene, on the coast of Sweden, north of Gottenburg, and the device was found engraved on metal objects discovered by Dr. Schlieman at Mycenæ.

Mr. Allen states that it also bears great resemblance to the "swastica" emblem of the Buddhists. The device is so peculiar, he says, that there can be little doubt as to the common origin of both the device on the stone at Ilkley, and that at Tossene, and indeed of the very numerous examples found at Troy. The only modification of form being that the arms of the former are curved instead of being angular. This "swastica" or "fyllot," is said to be a symbol of Baal or Woden; it is also used by the Chinese for the numeral 10,000, called in Chinese "Wan," and "on account of its

highly ornamental character, formed the element from which many
of their most elaborate decorative patterns were derived." The
design is also found in connection with the interlaced ornaments of
manuscripts and sculptured crosses in Great Britain. Mr. Allen
reminds us that :—" The special curved form of the "swastica"
from Ilkley, is well known to schoolboys as the solution of the following puzzle :—Four rich men and four poor men had their houses
symmetrically situated at the corners of two squares, one inside
the other, with a pond in the centre. The rich men determined
to build a wall which should exclude the poor men, who had their
houses close to the water, from the use of it, and at the same time
allow the rich men free access as before. How was this done ? "

Holmberg delineates as many as a hundred and sixty-five groups
of Swedish rock-cuttings, embracing all manner of devices taken
from ideas suggested by various forms of animal life, domestic and
warlike implements, geometrical shapings and other eccentric and
inexplicable forms. Some rocks are covered with markings of
crosses, single and double, circles enclosing crosses or plain, and
signs like those of the Zodiac and those employed by the alchym-
ists and seekers after the philosopher's stone. Boat-like configurations, closely resembling the gondolas of Venice, either empty or
conveying passengers, are found in numbers. Men raising or throw-
ing spears, and shooting arrows from bows are found. Several rocks
are literally covered with grotesque animals, some represented as
exceedingly bulky, with horns like cows, and others as quite the
opposite, thin and attenuated. In another place we have some very
regularly executed facsimiles of wheels with eight spokes, and so
on, the boat form perhaps predominating, as is not at all unnatural
in connection with rocks found either near or actually upon the
coast.

In Dr. Keller's Lake Dwellings of Switzerland (translated by Mr.
J. C. Lee) we have an account of certain cupped stones discovered
in that country. These are described as amongst the most remarkable antiquities of Swiss ownership, and as having been found by
the lake of Neuchatel, at Corcelettes, at Font, above Estavayer,
and at the lake dwellings of Cortaillod, just opposite the shore, almost always in places which are dry at low water.

" The implements met with in the neighbourhood of these hollow stones belong in general to the bronze age. The cups vary from
3 to 10 inches in diameter ; they are seldom more than an inch in
depth. They are made on the surface of the stone without any
kind of order, except that when they are three in number they form

as it were, the points of an equilateral triangle. The number of hollows or cups varies exceedingly; sometimes as in the stones found in the lake dwellings above mentioned, there is only one, but more frequently there are from ten to twenty. A stone in the collection of Colonel Schwab, weighing about five hundred weight, is remarkable for having on one side a single hollow a foot in diameter, and on the other side, eight smaller hollows. These stones do not show the least trace of work except the cups; they are all made out of erratic blocks, and chiefly of granite, or some other very hard stone.

"In the neighbourhood of Bienne, 'im-Luterholz,' on an exposed eminence, there is a block weighing about twenty hundredweight, with eighteen hollows, of which eight are set in pairs, and six in rows of three, joined together by furrows. Another was found in a grave opened on the height of Jolimont, between the lakes of Bienne and Neuchatel."

CHAPTER VII.

Rock Markings in Brazil.

SCHOLARS and antiquarians have deplored the fact that the antiquities of Brazil have received up to the present time, comparatively little attention. The neglect they attribute to the general rarity of the relics, and the difficulty of exploring the country. Professor Hartt, however, has devoted a considerable amount of attention to the curiosities of the Amazonas, a region he had opportunities of exploring in the summer of the year 1870, and to him chiefly we are indebted for what we know of the rock-markings of that part of our world.

On the Rio Tocantins near the lower falls, figures in considerable numbers were found, some engraved and others painted, all being of an extremely rude description. Many were also found in the Serra of Obidas, and on the Rio Oyapock.

The Tocantins inscriptions occurred at Alcobaca, a point on the left bank of the river, near the first falls, and about one hundred miles from the mouth of the river. Here are exposed on the banks during the dry season, beds of a fine grained, very hard, dark red or brown quartzite, the strata having only a slight dip. Joints divide the beds into large blocks, which often lie in place, but along a part of the shore they are piled up in confusion. During several months of the year, when the river is high, the locality is under water, as is the case with similar incised rocks at Serpa, on the Amazonas. Professor Hartt's guide told him that here were *letreiros,* or Indian inscriptions, and he says he was fortunate enough, not only to find several, but to be able to bring away with him two small incised blocks. He found the figures had been pecked into the rock by means of some blunt pointed instrument. They were so rude and irregular, that he saw no reason why a pointed stone might not have answered the purpose. " The grooves were usually wide and not very deep. Occasionally," he says, " the unskilled hand missed its mark and marred the figure. The figures were usually cut on the sides of the blocks of rock, and showed much wear ; many were hard to trace, and the majority were more or less covered by a shining black film of manganese deposited by the water."

The inscriptions on these rocks are of a somewhat diversified as well as complicated character, and many of them are not easy to describe merely by the tongue or pen. One, some sixteen inches in length, is that of a decapitated human figure, apparently in the act of jumping, with the arms raised. Spirals more or less complicated, abound, some being evidently intended to represent the human face, though so rudely executed as to be sometimes difficult of identification. On some of the sandstone rocks, a short distance from where the above are found, are places worn by grinding. Some of these, the Professor says, are circular, about a foot in diameter, quite shallow, and with a convex prominence in the middle, showing that a tool, probably a stone axe, had been ground with a circular motion. Others were shallow, oval hollows, a foot or more in length, made by rubbing the tool backward and forward. He saw also, a long, narrow, and rather deep groove, worn in the same way, perhaps, he conjectures, in the grinding of arrow heads. "These grinding surfaces," he continues, "looked to me totally unlike those made in sharpening metal tools. It is important to note that on the Tocantins, this is almost the only place where sandstones occur suitable for whetstones or grindstones; the locality would therefore be likely to be frequented by savages for the purpose of grinding and manufacturing stone implements."

Engraved figures occur elsewhere in Brazil, on the lower part of the Rio de Sao Francisco, in the Province Parahyba, on the Rio Negro, etc.

On the northern side of the valley of the Amazonas, some fifteen miles from the main river, a short distance from the Rio Gurupatuba, is the Serra do Ereré. It is a narrow, very irregular ridge, about 800 feet high, running nearly east and west, and about four or five miles long. The rock is sandstone in very heavy beds, inclined to the south-eastward. These sandstones form a broken line of cliffs running along the western side near the top, below which is a very irregular rocky slope. On these walls of rock, at and near the western end of the Serra, sometimes near their base, sometimes high up in conspicuous situations difficult of access, are great numbers of rude characters and figures, for the most part in red paint, some isolated, others in groups. Some rock surfaces are thickly covered with them, many being so washed by rains and defaced by fires as not to be traced out, others being brought out fresh, suggesting that they were not all executed at the same time. Standing just in advance of the line of cliffs at some distance east of the western end of the Serra, is a tall, tower like mass of sandstone

painted not only on the base, but high up on the sides, while the
cliffs behind and on both sides are covered with figures. All the
localities are very conspicuous, and some of them are so large as to
be visible at the distance of more than a mile.

Not far from the eastern end of the Serra there is on top an
enormous isolated mass of sandstone, the remains of a bed almost
entirely removed, which mass is distinctly visible from the plain
below on the northern side. The irregular western wall of this
mass is covered with figures.

Here again we find, as in other places, considerable diversity in
the figures. Conspicuous amongst them are seen representations
of the sun, moon, and stars. At the western end of Ereré, on the
cliff near the top, is a rude circular figure, nearly two feet in diameter, of a brownish yellow colour, having in the centre a large
red spot, the circumference being a broad border of the same
colour. Some of the Indians call this the sun, others call it the
moon. Some distance east of this, is another prominent cliff, having a similar figure almost three feet in diameter. In this there is
a central spot of brick red, then a broad zone of a dirty yellow,
followed by a zone of brick red, outside of which is another of a
dirty ochre yellow. To the right of this are two smaller circular
figures, in the upper of which the lines and centre are red, the innermost zone being of a dirty yellow tint. These figures are situated some ten feet from the foot of the cliff. Similar drawings
composed of two or more concentric circles, with or without the
central spot, occur in great numbers at Ereré. Professor Hartt
says he is disposed to think that they are intended to represent the
moon, since they are not furnished with rays. One figure on the
cliff at the western end of the Serra, undoubtedly represents this
heavenly body. Besides the above forms there are rayed figures
in abundance. Sometimes they consist of a single circle or several
concentric circles, the outer one, only, being rayed, but on the
side of the great rock on the top of the Serra is a figure a foot in
diameter, and very distinct, formed of two concentric circles, each
with a few large tooth shaped rays. Part of this figure is obliterated. At the same locality is another figure consisting of a circle
with serrated rays with only a spot in the centre. There are also
circles, single and double, sometimes nucleated, which bear rays
only on the upper side ; and rayed spirals, some of which appear
to represent stars, some of which are drawn, and others engraved.
Some of the figures are rude and grotesque in the extreme ; one,
about three feet six inches high looks like the sun with a human

body ; another at the western end of the Serra is a curious rayed head, ornamented at the top with what looks very much like a comet. Animals of various kinds are also depicted as well as the human form and the sun, moon, and stars. At the west end of the Serra is the figure of a snake ; in another place is seen what the Indians call a *mucura*, a species of opossum, and others supposed to represent alligators. Birds are very seldom seen, a few markings only which may be taken for such being found. Several drawings of the sea cow exist, and a few of fishes ; none of the dog, ox, or horse. A very large number of the cuttings and paintings are too mystical to give any meaning whatever to, and appear like the productions of mere children.

Professor Hartt says :—" The antiquity of the rock paintings and sculptures of Eastern South America is undoubted, and they are mentioned by many of the ancient writers, as well as by Humboldt, and others in more recent times. It is well known that the drawings of Ereré, and those of Obidos, existed more than two hundred years ago. There can be no doubt that they antedate the civilization of the Amazonas, and there is a strong probability that some of them, at least, were drawn before the discovery of America. I hold it most probable that the rock paintings and sculpturings were made by tribes which inhabited the Amazonas previous to the Tupi invasion. The sculpturings are supposed to be older than the paintings. This is also, I believe, the opinion of Senhor Penna. I think the Ereré figures have a deep significance. A people that would go to so much trouble as to draw figures of the sun and moon high up on cliffs on the tops of mountains must have attached a great importance to these natural objects, and I think that these figures point to worship of the sun by the tribes which executed them. The clustering of the inscriptions in prominent places, and especially on and in the vicinity of the rock tower of Ereré, seem to me to indicate that these places had something of a sacred character and were often resorted to. Many of the figures seem to be the capricious daubings of visitors, as, for instance, the human faces drawn on angular rock projections.

" I know of no trace of sun-worship among the uncivilized Indians of Para to-day, nor do they make rock paintings or inscriptions. The greater part of the Brazilian Indians, such as the Tupis, Botocudas, etc., appear to have had no idea of a God, and no form of worship. We have no historical account of the practice of sun-worship among the ancient Indians of the Amazonas. The probabilities are, that the tribes anciently inhabiting the Amazonas were more advanced in religious ideas than those Brazilian Indians of which history gives us an account."

A number of rock inscriptions equally eccentric with those of other nations, have been found in Brazil, and have been described and pictured by Mr. J. C. Branner in the pages of the American Naturalist. He tells us that in 1876, he visited Aguas Bellas, a small town in the interior of the Province of Pernambuco, and about a hundred miles from the coast, for the purpose of examining localities said to contain the remains of extinct animals. The fossils were found at and in the vicinity of a cattle ranch, known as Lagôa da Lagea, eight leagues east of Aguas Bellas. During the time spent at this place, he says he heard of several rocks in the vicinity bearing inscriptions which, it was said, no man could read. He took time to visit the most convenient of these localities, and made careful drawings of the markings. The first place he visited for this purpose was a small farm about a league from Lagôa du Lagea, known as Cacimba Circada. The rock found at this place was a gneiss boulder, about 10 ft. by 6 ft., and 6 ft. in thickness.

On the right as the inscription was faced, was an asterisk a foot in diameter, made by four lines crossing each other at equal angles, while the remainder of the inscription on the left, consisted of three rows of marks or indentations that ran down from near the top of the rock about two and a half feet to where a portion of the block had split off from the lower left corner, probably carrying away part of the inscription. It was impossible to determine the exact number of these points, for some of them, especially those near the top, had become very indistinct through the weathering of the face of the rock. The inscriptions appeared to have been made by pecking with stone implements, and in the case of the asterisk, the stone was rubbed up and down the line until the furrows were well polished. After being ground out, these points and lines were painted, the colour having at the time of this description, a dull red or brown appearance.

The next place visited was Pedra Pintada (painted stone) which is located upon a stream (during the rainy season) taking its name from the marked stones—Rio da Pedra Pintada. There are here about forty designs engraved, and part of them both engraved and painted upon the large block of the gneiss on the banks, and upon the flat smooth rock in the dry bed of the stream. There is a cascade about twenty-five feet high here, and at the foot of it a pothole, now filled up, which is about fifteen feet wide by as many deep, and to the presence of which these inscriptions are possibly due. The engraving appears to have been done like that at Cacimba Circada, by pecking and grinding with stones having thin rounded edges. After being thus polished, these marks were painted, the colour now shewing as a dull red or brown. In some cases the points and lines are combined as is shewn in the drawings. The arrangement of points in parallel vertical lines is rather frequent, occurring several times here, as well as at Cacimba Circada, and at Sant' Anna. There are two asterisks of eight rays, one associated with other markings, and another one independent, while still another asterisk has twenty rays. The only figure that seems to be intended to represent anything is one which appears to be a rude representation of a spear head. One might be supposed to represent a fish, but the resemblance may be accidental. The resemblance of some of these designs and some given by Professor Hartt from the Amazon region is noteworthy, especially that of a spiral, and one of a circle with the point at the centre.

Returning from Aguas Bellas to the Rio Sao Francisco, by way of the village of Sant' Anna, in the province of Alagoas, at half a league from this latter place, Mr. Branner found a number of figures inscribed upon the side of a large gneiss boulder of decomposition. These figures—crescents, circles, small curves, angles, and straight lines thick at one end and gradually tapering to points at the other —were both cut and painted, and had the same dull red colour as those at Pedra Pintada. There were other marks upon the vertical faces of this and of the other boulders of the group, evidently made by the same hands. These were simply polished spots, varying in size from one to two feet in diameter. They were for the most part, nearly round, but some of them were oblong, and none of them were more than about a quarter of an inch in depth—most of them not so deep, all being painted. The stones upon which these inscriptions were made, as has already been stated, were gneiss boulders of decomposition, about a dozen in number, from 6 to 12 ft. in height, grouped together upon the summit of a little hill of solid gneiss.

Mr. Branner proceeds to say :—" It should be noted that these inscriptions, as well as many others which I heard of through this part of the country, are all upon these large stones, and generally in some such prominent place. One inscription in particular was mentioned to me by several persons, all of whom gave substantially the same account of it. This inscribed rock is near Agua Branca, twelve leagues above Piranhas, and ten leagues from the falls of

Paulo Affonso, on the *Fazenda da Caisara*, and is known as the *pedra navio*, or ship-stone. It is said to be a large and nearly round boulder, standing upon a very narrow base upon the solid rock, and to have all its sides covered with Indian inscriptions. Through this part of the country, where the archæan rocks form a wide belt between the plateaus of the interior, and the Cretaceous and Tertiary beds near the coast, these boulders of decomposition are not uncommon, and almost everyone that I have seen has had some sort of artificial marks upon it, generally too badly eroded to be defined, but sufficiently distinct to leave no doubt concerning their origin."

Mr. Branner says of the figures themselves he is unable to suggest any definite explanation. Those given by the people in the vicinity throw no light upon the subject. Some think they were made by the Dutch when they held the country about Pernambuco in the early part of the seventeenth century, but the general impression is that they refer to some treasure hidden in the neighbourhood. This idea led a former proprietor of the country about Pedra Pintada to make a diligent search for this supposed treasure, and he even cleared out the great pot-hole at the foot of the cascade, but without finding anything.

"It is to be noted, however, as far as I have observed, that these inscriptions are always near the water, or near a place where water is likely to be found late in, if not quite through the dry season. At Pedra Pintada the pot-hole below the fall has water in it long after the stream proper has dried up, the Ipanema has never been known to dry up entirely at Sant' Anna, while Cacimba Circada (fenced spring) takes its name from a spring at that place. This occurrence of the inscriptions in the neighbourhood of water, might admit of more than one explanation. If they have no other relation to the water itself, they happen to be in these localities, because these are the places where the original inhabitants of the country would naturally live during the dry season, which is here nearly half the year, and indeed a part of these inscriptions at least—those in the bed of the stream—must have been made during the dry season. I am, however, inclined to the opinion that a part, if not all, of these markings refer in some way to the water supply which is so uncertain in this region of great drouths. Exactly in what way, whether as records of seasons, or as petitions or offerings to the powers supposed to bring rain, it is idle now to speculate. To one visiting this section during the dry season, which lasts from August to January, there is no more natural explanation. The

whole country is parched except the cacti and a very narrow strip
bordering the now dry beds of the streams. Beyond those threads
of gradually disappearing green, one may travel for leagues and
leagues without seeing a sign of water, and when, as not unfrequently happens, the dry season is prolonged, the suffering to man
and beast is extreme. The cattle subsist upon the pulp of the cacti
that grow here abundantly, while the herdsmen obtain water for
them by digging holes in the sand of the river beds wherever water
may be found in this manner. If the drouth still continues beyond
this stage, the cattle are driven toward the coast to where water
may be had, or they are left to perish of thirst.

" Without experience of such circumstances it is, perhaps, not easy
to realise the force of the argument, but after riding for days through
this region, with a tropical sun blazing overhead, the atmosphere
so dry that it seems to parch one's very vitals, and the heat from
the glaring white sand quivering upwards to a cloudless sky, the
thin catinga forest shrivelled and still, with not a sigh of animal
life, save the metallic stridulation of an occasional grasshopper, and
after passing now and then a whole day without water, one realizes
the importance which savage races, dwelling in such a country,
would attach to a stream or pool where water could be had during
the dry season."

CHAPTER VIII.

Rock Markings in North America.

AMERICAN inscriptions are of two kinds or classes.

1.—Those in Gothic, Hebrew, or other recognised languages. By some, these are ascribed to ancient colonists, and by others denounced as modern forgeries.

2.—Those of unknown characters, or partly unknown, found mostly on rocks in distant and divers parts of the county. Such only can safely be attributed to the red race. But as a few rude figures bear resemblance to letters, they present an enigma which some have solved, or thought to solve, by assigning to them comparatively modern dates. The decision may be right, but the test is unphilosophical and unreliable. It does not follow that an inscription must be of civilised origin because some of its characters resemble letters in Eastern writings, nor yet that ancient like characters in modern inscriptions are derived from the ancients. Another proposition is, that American aborigines had no conception of phonetic symbols; hence, inscriptions on which such occur are either foreign or forged. The strongest proof of the Grave Creek pebble not being of Indian origin, would be its characters yielding intelligent information as symbols of sounds. They are arranged in three parallel lines, as in a book, but there is nothing like that observable on rocks; on the contrary, the figures generally present a jumble of groups and single marks that appear to have little connexion with each other, as if the work of individuals on different times and occasions. There is, in truth, no more resemblance between North American rock writing and inscriptions of Assyria and the East, than between a child's unintelligible scrawls on paper and a printed page. Indians have always made significant marks on various substances, and occasionally on diverse implements. "Even on a celt or axe," says Mr. Ewbank, " I see nothing strange in its owner thus distinguishing a favourite tool or weapon from mere fancy, if not from a more serious motive. Why not it as well as his war club, paddle and pipe? Are not sword-blades ornamented with etchings, and did not Eastern warriors have devices engraved on their battle axe blades? Without proof or strong indications of fraud, I would rather attribute the marks to caprice than deception ; for such a solution, lame as it may be, would accord with that of Capt. B. Romans, who visited the Floridas in 1771—2, and published his account of them in 1776. He mentions among other things, stones deeply marked with straight and crossed lines, which, says he, " do not ill resemble inscriptions," but conjectures they were made by the savages in grinding their awls. Whether these were iron or steel substitutes for bone bodkins used in making their mocassins, and sewing skins, we are not informed, nor is it material. Pointed instruments are sharpened in straight grooves. Anything like an inscribed stone in which they cross each other in every direction, would be the worst kind of whetstone for the purpose. He admits that they fairly resembled inscriptions, but was not prepared to acknowledge them as such, probably because incompatible with his ideas of the savage state, and his settled conviction that God created an Adam and Eve expressly for this part of the earth, and peopled it with quite a different species from other men and women."

Notwithstanding arbitrary and ideographic characters date far behind prehistoric ages, and have been and are more or less common with barbarians and semi-barbarians, there is a disposition to conclude that those of the Red Race have been got, some way or other, from civilized sources ; as if the inventive instinct was not common to every race, and as if the seeds of important discoveries were not sown in the rudest ages. The characters and their application to transmit information are natural suggestions ; they have been the resource of uneducated men everywhere, and are so still, even in enlightened lands. Who has not heard of litigations arising from them among the early settlers on the Hudson and Mohawk ? A chalked ring, was, in country stores, a common representation of a cheese, one of which being charged to a farmer instead of a grindstone, led to an acrimonious dispute, the clerk having omitted to mark a hole in the centre—an illustration of wrangles common to all people before symbolic gave way to phonetic signs.

American, like other aborigines, must of necessity have originated their signs. None else could have been understood. But, it is said, resemblances to letters are so obvious as to suggest a common origin. This, Mr. Ewbank submits, is a common error. " Try it," he says, " by applying the same reasoning to other things—to such as with equal reason it may be applied—and the inference must be, that the indigines of this half of the earth are indebted to the other half for the bow and arrow, the sling, club and canoe. I

F

would as soon imagine the habits and instincts of animals of one country derived from those of another as that these characters or signs must have come from abroad. Communication of thought by them is more readily developed than ensnaring animals, catching fish, spinning and weaving, vessels of earthenware and heating water. The resemblances are, I believe, as innocent of imitation as any inborn device whatever—they are coincidences which might be expected and hardly to be avoided. It would be remarkable if similitudes and occasional facsimiles did not occur, for it may be doubted if half a dozen lines of new characters can be produced that would not afford ground for ingenuity to show, with much plausibility, the derivation of more or less of them from alphabets.

" I suppose there is scarcely an Indian sign on rock, tree, bark, skin, wood or bone, that may not be thought to afford ground for zealous theorists to suspect imitation. Of some rather common, there is a circle, and yet who in his right mind would say it was derived from the letter O, a half circle from C or D, a straight line from I, another joined to it at right angles from an L or T, or acutely joined from a V, and so we might proceed with N and W, N and Z, X, &c., to the arrow headed, and the common musical character, found more or less distinct on rocks. There is hardly a tribal mark painted on the face of a savage, or tatooed on his person, but the germ of some European or Oriental letter might be imagined in it." *

Of inscriptions seen by early travellers, one of decided interest is mentioned by Professor Calm who made a tour in Canada in 1748—50, under the patronage of the king, and University of Sweden. After speaking of the entire absence of ruins or evidence of ancient habitations, he says :—" There have, however, been found a few marks of antiquity, from which it may be inferred that North America was formerly inhabited by a nation more versed in science and more civilized than that which the Europeans found here on their arrival ; or that a great military expedition was undertaken to this continent from those unknown parts of the world." He then states that some years before he came into Canada, the Governor sent a party across the continent to the South Sea. On their way, they came to a place in the woods about nine hundred French miles west of Montreal, where were large pillars of stone leaning upon each other, so large that the Frenchmen could not suppose they had been erected by human hands. They also met

---

* Historical Magazine.

with a large stone or pillar in which a smaller stone was fixed and covered on both sides with unknown characters. It was about a French foot in length, and between four and five inches broad. It was taken to Canada and sent thence to France. Jesuits who saw the stone pronounced the characters Tartarian.

In the autumn of 1871, the subject of rock inscriptions in Ohio came under the special notice of the American Association for the Advancement of Science, by the introduction to that body of a number of diagrams, and the reading of a paper by Col. C. Whittlesey. From the report in the American Naturalist we learn that the largest was a tracing made by Dr. J. H. Salisbury, of Cleveland, with the assistance of Mrs. Salisbury, from a mural face of conglomerate, near the famous " Black Hand " in Licking County. Once there was a space of ten or twelve feet in height, by fifty or sixty feet in length, covered by these inscriptions. Most of them have been obliterated by the recent white settlers.

" In 1861, Dr. Salisbury took copies from a space about eight by fifteen feet, by laying a piece of coarse muslin over them, and tracing such as remain uninjured, life-size, on the cloth. In this space there are found to be twenty-three characters, most of which are the arrow-head or bird-track character. These are all cut on the edge of the strata, presenting a face nearly vertical, but a little shelving outward, so as to be sheltered by the weather.

Another copy of the remnant of similar inscriptions was taken by Col. Whittlesey and Mr. J. B. Comstock, in 1869, from the "Turkey Foot Rock," at the rapids of the Maumee, near Perrysburg. These are on a block of limestone, and in the course of the twenty-five past years have been nearly destroyed by the hand of man. What is left was taken by a tracing of the size of nature.

On the surface of a quarry of grindstone grit at Independence, Cuyahoga County, Ohio, a large inscribed surface was uncovered in 1854. Mr. B. Wood, Deacon Bicknell, and other citizens of Independence, secured a block about six feet by four, and built it into the north wall of a stone church they were then building. Col. Whittlesey presented a reduced sketch, one-fourth size of nature, taken by Dr. Salisbury and Dr. J. M. Lewis, in 1869, which was made perfect by the assistance of a photographer. Some of the figures sculptured on this slab are cut an inch to an inch and a half in the rock, and they were covered by soil a foot to eighteen inches in thickness, on which large trees were growing. Like all of the others, they were made by a sharp pointed tool like a pick, but as yet no such tool has been found among the relics of the

mound-builders or of the Indians. The figures are very curious.
Among them is something like a trident, or fish-spear, a serpent, a
human hand, and a number of track-like figures, which the people
call buffalo tracks, but Dr. Salisbury regards as a closer representation of a human foot covered by a shoe-pack or mocassin.
Another figure somewhat resembles the section of a bell with its
clapper.

Near the west line of Belmont County, Ohio, Mr. James W.
Ward, then of Cincinnatti, now of New York, in 1859, took a sketch
of two large isolated sandstone rocks, on which are groups of
figures similar to those already noticed. Here are the bird-track
characters, the serpent, the mocassin or buffalo tracks, and some
anomalous figures. These are plainly cut with a pick, into the
surface of the rock, which, like the Independence stone, is substantially imperishable. Here we have also the representation of the
human foot, and the foot of a bear. Another figure, which appears
to be the foot of some animal with four clumpy toes, Professor
Cope thinks may be the foretrack of a Menopome. One peculiarity
of these sculptured human feet is a monstrously enlarged great
toe-joint, even greater than is produced by the modern process of
shoe-pinching. This has been observed in other ancient carvings
of the human foot upon the rocks near St. Louis, Missouri. These
feet range in size from seven to fifteen inches in length. Of all
these representatives the bear's foot is closest to nature. The bird-
track, so called, presents six varieties, none of which are anatomi-
cally correct. The human hand is more perfect than the foot.

Dr. Salisbury finds, on comparison of these symbolical figures
with the Oriental sign-writing, or hieroglyphical alphabets, that
there are many characters in common. Some 800 years before
Christ, the Chinese had a bird-track character in their syllable
alphabet. The serpent is a symbol so common among the early
nations, and has a significance so various, that very little use can
be made of it in the comparison.

These inscriptions differ materially from those made by the
modern red man. He is unable to read that class of them which
appears to be ancient.

Lieut. Whipple has mentioned in the "Government Report on
the Pacific Railroad Surveys," an instance of the bird-track character inscribed upon the rocks of Arizona. Professor Kerr, of North
Carolina, states that he has noticed similar characters cut in the
rocks of one of the passes of the Black Mountains, at the head of
the Tennessee river.

" These facts indicate wide spread universality in the use of this style of inscription, and it indicates something higher than the present symbolical or picture writing of the North American Indians."

The American Naturalist for 1885 supplies us with some interesting notes relative to certain " Rock Inscriptions on the Lake of the Woods, from the pen of Mr. A. C. Lawson."

This locality is described in the *Gazetteers*, as a large lake of North America near latitude 49° N. It is partly in Minnesota, and partly in Keewatin, Canada. It has an irregular form, nearly 100 miles long, and 250 miles or more in circuit. It is supplied by Rainy Lake River, and the surplus water is discharged by the Winnipeg River, which issues from the north end of the lake. Mr. Lawson says :— " The Lake of the Woods is divided about its middle into two parts, a northern and a southern, by a large peninsula extending from the neck of land at Turtle Portage on the east side of the lake to within a very few miles of the west shore. On the north side of this peninsula, *i.e.*, on the south shore of the northern half of the lake, about midway between the east and west shores, occurs one of two sets of hieroglyphic markings, which, while prosecuting a general survey of the lake, I observed upon the rocks." A drawing supplied by the writer shows that these markings consisted of such forms as spirals, circles within circles, crosses, triangles, arrows, horse-shoe like shapes, the Greek P.H., etc. " Lying off shore at a distance of a quarter to half a mile, and making with it a long sheltered channel, is a chain of islands trending east and west. On the south side of one of these islands, less than a mile to the west of the first locality, is to be seen the other set of inscriptions. The first set occurs on the top of a low, glaciated, projecting point of rock which presents the characters of an ordinary roche moutonnée. The rock is a very soft, foliated, green, chloritic schist, into which the characters are more or less deeply carved. The top of the rounded point is only a few feet above the high water mark of the lake, whose waters rise and fall in different seasons through the range of ten feet. The antiquity of the inscriptions is at once forced upon the observer upon a careful comparison of their weathering, with that of the glacial grooves and striæ, which are very distinctly seen upon the same rock surface. Both the ice grooves and carved inscriptions are, so far as the eye can judge, identical in extent of weathering, though there was doubtless a considerable lapse of time between the disappearance of the glaciers and the date of the carving. The ice grooves are not merely local scratches, but part of the regular striation which characterizes the whole region. Both the striæ and inscriptions present a marked contrast to some recent letters which passing traders or travellers, attracted by the novelty of the inscriptions, have cut into the rock, much in the same spirit as that in which my Christianized Indian canoe-man proceeded to carve his initials in the rock with my hammer the moment we landed. The weathered and rough character of the carving afforded no clue as to the tool used. In size the characters varied from about three to twelve inches. There was no indication of ochre having been rubbed into the carving. The characters were scattered over the rock surface in all directions and in great numbers. The chief advantage to be derived by archæologists from an acquaintance with such inscriptions is the tracing out the similarity or identity of the individual characters with those of inscriptions found in other parts of the continent. There is little hope of any coherent meaning or narrative ever being derived from such isolated groups of characters."

The writer then proceeds to point out certain very striking points of similarity between these markings and those described by Mr. Branner from the boulders of Alagoas. This, in many instances, is so distinct, that, as he says—" There is no need of straining the comparison." The coincidence appears to be too strong to be purely accidental, although considering the remoteness of the two regions in question, much more abundant material for comparison would be required before inferences, even of the most general sort, could be drawn.

" The island on which were found the other inscriptions to which I have alluded, is one of the many steep rocky islands known among the Indians as Ka-ka-ki-wa-bic min-nis, or Crow-rock island. The rock is a hard greenstone, not easily cut, and the inscriptions are not cut into the rock, but are painted with ochre, which is much faded in places. The surface upon which the characters are inscribed forms an overhanging wall protected from the rain, part of which has fallen down, cutting off the inscription sharply. The Indians of the present day have no traditions about these inscriptions beyond the supposition that they must have been made by the ' old people long ago.' "

CHAPTER IX.

Rock Markings in India and Australia.

A CORRESPONDENT of *Notes and Queries* (H. Rivett-Carnac) writting in 1877, says:—"I first came across the 'cup-markings,' or Sir J. Simpson's 'first type,' on the boulders of the stone circles or barrows in the Nagpore country of the Central Provinces, or, in fact, on exactly the same class of remains as those on which similar markings are found in the north of England, Scotland, Ireland, and other parts of Europe. These barrows and their contents have often been described by writers on Indian Antiquarian subjects, by the late Rev. S. Hislop, Colonel Meadows Taylor, and others : but the existence of the 'cup marks' apparently escaped their notice. These marking were briefly described by me at a meeting of the Asiatic Society of Bengal, held, I think, early in 1872. But I am now travelling among the Himalayas ; and as my baggage is necessarily confined to what can be carried on the backs of a limited number of men, I have no books of reference with me, and cannot give the exact date.

" During an autumn holiday amongst these glorious mountains, I have had the good fortune to come across a rock at a point near Chandeshwur, about twelve and a half miles north of the military station of Rainbhet, which, on examination, proved to be profusely sculptured with several of the types described by Sir J. Simpson.

" Thus I found upwards of two hundred of the ordinary 'cup-marks' arranged in various permutations ; also 'cup marks' enclosed within circles, and circles with 'gutters,' and markings corresponding nearly exactly with figs. 1 and 15 of plate 2 of Sir J. Simpson's work.

" The markings are undoubtedly old, and no local tradition exists concerning them, beyond a vague story that they must be the work of the 'giants,' or of the Goalee dynastry ('the shepherd kings') who are supposed to have held rule in many parts of India before the advent of Ayran civilization.

" In the yard of the Lingam temple of Chandeshwur, at the mouth of the gorge in which the rock bearing these markings is situated, I come upon some forty or fifty small shrines, surmounted by representations of the Lingam and Yoni. On the better class of shrines, the solid stone yoni, with cylindrical lingams of the well known type, was to be found ; but the greater part were marked by much rougher and poorer representations of the same symbols. On slabs split off from the adjacent rocks, were carved two circles with a "gutter" in the centre, the inner circle taking the place of the cylindrical ling, the outer circle that of the yoni. The outer was intersected by the ' gutter,' which is common to the symbols, large and small, and seems to be for the purpose of carrying off the libations of holy water, with which pilgrims and worshippers sprinkle their shrines profusely. These rough symbols bear a striking resemblance to the markings on the rock close by, and to many of the markings figured in Sir J. Simpson's plates.

"It suggests itself, then, that the markings on the monoliths and rocks in Europe may also be connected with lingam worship. I am aware that Sir J. Simpson dismisses this idea as improbable. But the view taken by that eminent authority seems to have been chiefly founded on the absence of anatomical resemblance. I am sanguine that if Sir J. Simpson had lived to see sketches of the Chandeshwur markings, and of what I will call the conventional markings used in the temple close by to represent the lingam and yoni, he might, perhaps, have been inclined to modify that view. As a matter of fact, the stones which do duty for the lingam and yoni on an Indian shrine, seldom bear more than the faintest anatomical resemblance to what they are intended to represent ; and the uninitiated may see them over and over again without supecting what they are meant for. The two circles with a gutter, found on the poorer class of shrines at Chandeshwur, are undoubtedly intended to represent the same symbols that are found on the better class of shrines in the same enclosure. The incisions on the poorer class are what I may call a conventional rendering of the symbols ; and the form adopted owes its origin in all probability to the circumstance that a ' ground plan ' of these symbols can be more conveniently carved than a ' section.'

"A few days after my visit to Chandeshwur, I climbed to the summit of the Pandu Koli hill, some eight thousand feet above the sea level, ten miles to the north east. There I found a lingam shrine, composed of two circles of stones, with several monolith lings in the centre of the inner circle. The little shrine was open to the elements on all sides, save where it was partially sheltered by a wild guelder rose, to the branches of which votive offerings of shreds of cloth had been attached by many pilgrims."

Some time after writing the above, the author alluding again to the cup marks in India, said :—" It was suggested that the permutations of large and small cups might be a primitive style of writing or inscription, after the manner of permutations of dots and strokes in the Morse system of primitive printing by electric telegraph. The paper by M. Terrien de Lacouperie, Journal of Royal Asiatic Society, Vol. XIV., seems to confirm this view, and notices the similarity of the Kumaon cup marks, and the ' Ho,' map of the Chinese 'Agh King.' It seems desirable then that antiquaries should carefully note such permutations."

In March 1879, Sir Charles Nicholson, Bart., LL.D., read a paper before the Anthropological Institute of Great Britain and Ireland, in reference to some rock carvings found in the neighbourhood of Sydney. He said that in various localities along the coast of New Holland, especially on the eastern side extending from Cape Howe to Moreton Bay, carvings are found on the surface of rocks, representing in low relief the human figure, portions of the human body, as the hand or foot ; and various animals, such as the kangaroo and whale. " The spots selected for the tracing of these outlines," he remarked, " are the sides and shelving roofs of open caves, but more generally the smooth horizontal surface of the rock itself at points near the edge of the cliffs overhanging the sea, or forming the boundaries of the different inlets by which the coast line is broken in various places along its eastern face. On the rocks overhanging the harbour of Port Jackson, and along the countless bays into which its waters spread ; at Broken Bay and the estuary of the Hawkesbury River, these remains are discoverable and are often only brought to light when the soil which has accumulated on the surface, and the vegetable growths by which they are concealed are removed. As not only brushwood, but large trees of considerable age are often found rooted in the soil that conceals these carvings, a considerable interval must have elapsed since the period when they were executed."

Some of these carvings, drawings of which were exhibited to the meeting, were discovered by Colonel Vigors, whilst engaged in superintending the erection of a battery at Middle Head, Port Jackson. " On clearing away the superficial soil and brushwood preparatory to the levelling of the rock, the carvings were brought to light. Exact measurements of the various objects were then made, and carefully reduced according to a given scale."

Colonel Vigors, in a communication addressed to Sir Charles Nicholson, said :—" The sandstone rock is formed into large horizontal tables, and on these the outlines were cut. They were

covered with several inches of vegetable mould." One was a specimen of the human figure, the only one of the kind discovered.
" One," the Colonel said, " he regarded with peculiar interest, as
showing the manner in which the natives began the work. Small
holes were drilled or made in the rock at intervals of a few inches
and were subsequently joined into one continuous line. One was
30 feet in length, and no doubt was meant to represent a whale."

Sir Charles says he has little to add to these remarks, except
that he has himself seen many similar examples of these " graphiti"
on the escarpments and surface of the rocks adjacent to the locality
from whence the drawings were derived. "Among the latter," he
proceeds, " I have no doubt the Dogong and other varieties of the
Phocæ are meant to be indicated by the aboriginal sculptor, as these
form a very important article of food to all the native tribes living
on the coast. A very common form of the carving here referred to
is one representing the human hand or foot. As to the age of these
remains it is difficult to form any opinion. From the extent of the
erosion to which these have been subjected, which have been exposed to the open air, as well as from the depth of the alluvium
and size of the trees by which the horizontal carvings are concealed,
it is evident that a very considerable interval must have elapsed
since the era of their production. The present native race can give
no account of these remains, and I think it will be generally admitted
that no aboriginal tribe, with whom any of the European inhabitants of Australia have been brought into contact, could have been
the authors of even such rudimentary examples of artistic skill.
Like other similar prehistoric carvings, found on the coasts of North
America and other parts of the world, they may be regarded as the
very earliest examples of the efforts of particular races of man to
give expression to the imitative faculty by way of pictorial design.

"At whatever period, and by whoever these and similar sculptures
were created, they are, I believe, the only real examples we have
of genuine Archaic Australian art. On the north west coast of
Australia, Sir George Gray discovered, many years since, some caves
on the sloping roof of one of which is painted on a black ground,
the rude form of a human figure in red and white, clothed with a
short tunic, and with the head surrounded by a sort of nimbus, like
that seen in mediæval pictures of Saints. Were it not for the
absence of the symbol of the cross, the figure here referred to might
be supposed to be a specimen of early Christian iconography.
There are also drawings in other adjacent caves of men carrying
kangaroos, and of various objects the nature of which it is not very

easy to divine, but which Sir George Gray suggests as representing implements of the chase. These chromatic pictorial representations found at the north west coast of Australia, are evidently of a wholly different character from the sculptured rocks described above. The localities where the painted figures are found are not very distant from those parts of the northern coast frequented by the Malays fishing for trepang and the pearl oyster, and holding more or less intercourse with the natives of the soil. I would venture to suggest the probability that the paintings discovered by Sir George Grey, and described by him in the account of his explorations in the north east of Australia may be the work of some accidental visitors, Malays, or possibly shipwrecked European sailors, attributable to some one belonging to a race distinct and superior to thatwhich, so far as observation has hitherto extended, has held exclusive possession of the vast territory of Australasia. That Europeans have occasionally been isolated or seized by the natives, and compelled to consort with them for a length of time, sufficient to obliterate nearly all the habits and associations of earlier civilized life, is well known to those acquainted with the history of the various colonies of Australia. When the first settlement from Van Diemen's Land was made in Victoria in 1836, an Englishman of the name of Berkley, was discovered living with one of the tribes of the Aborigines. He had left one of the penal settlements of the colony, had associated himself with the blacks, and for some thirty years had never seen the face of a white man. In this long interval he had lost, with the exception of a few words, the use of his native language, had dispensed with all clothing, and had conformed in every way to the habits of the race amongst whom his lot had been cast. The early habits of civilized life had, however, left a sufficient impress on his character to enable him to exercise a considerable ascendancy in the tribe to which he had attached himself. It is quite conceivable that such a man, during his enforced residence amongst savages, may have sought to preserve some of the earlier reminiscences of his life in rude pictorial representations, such as those described by Sir Charles Grey.

"With reference to the chiseled drawings, it must be admitted that they exhibit a degree of mechanical skill, and a sense of pictorial effect, that could only have belonged to a race considerably in advance of any now extant on the continent of New Holland. The existing aboriginal native of Australia presents one of the very lowest of all known types of humanity. Has there been any degradation from an earlier and somewhat higher standard ? Whatever conclusion we may come to on the subject, it is at all events interesting to recognize in these uncouth and infantile efforts of the savage to give permanent expression to the images that occupy his mind, the existence of a faculty and an instinct which have their highest development and influence in the most advanced stages of civilization." *

* Jour. Anthrop. Inst., v. IX.

CHAPTER X.

Execution and Signification of the Rock Markings.

DISCUSSING the kind of tool with which the rock markings were made—whether of stone or metal—Mr. Tate says :— " The markings have been chipped or picked out, and not made by rubbing; the best preserved figures show that the tool was bluntly pointed. All our sculptures are in sandstone, which could have been incised by such a tool as was used, in far distant pre-historic times, made of basalt, flint, moonstone, trap or jaspar. Metals, however, were known in the district when the sculptures were incised ; bronze and copper objects have been found in their neighbourhood ; and in some parts of North Northumberland considerable numbers of bronze celts have been discovered, as well as bronze daggers, spear heads, and swords. Querns made of hard intractable porphyry have been taken from the forts about Yevering, and one from the Weetwood Camp; but as these could not have been fashioned by any stone tool, it is therefore probable that metallic tools had been also used to inscribe the Northumberland rocks, which are so hard that stone tools could not have chipped out the inscriptions. Probably the metal was bronze, which seems to have been in considerable use at the period."

It is impossible to contemplate these mysterious markings, so widely spread over almost the entire world, but so strangely similar whether found in England, Ireland, Scotland, Central Europe, India, Australia, Switzerland, Sweden, or South America, without asking by whom were they made and what is their signification ? If they are merely ornamental, they are of course interesting—and some of them no doubt may fairly be thus described—but there is probably a deeper meaning attached to them which is not so easily arrived at.

Mr. Tate, in the year 1853, in opposition perhaps to the views promulgated by Mr. Greenwell, Dr. Johnson, and Sir Gardner Wilkinson, who had held that the cup and ring markings were plans of camps, advocated the notion that they were symbolical figures representing religious thoughts.

In his anniversary address to the members of the Berwickshire Naturalists' Club, at the meeting held at Embleton, September 7,

1853, he spoke of a visit which had been paid to Routin Linn in the spring of the same year by some of the members, when they had examined the various rock markings, and endeavoured to form some conjecture as to their origin, and proceeds :— "When learned doctors differ, or hesitate to give an opinion, it would be presumptuous in me to adjudicate. Indeed, if these sculpturings stood alone, the fear of Edie Ochiltree might scare any one from indulging in a conjecture ; but when viewed in connexion with other facts, some inferences may reasonably be drawn. That they are of great antiquity is proved by the depth of peaty soil which covers part of them, and which amounts, even on the slope of a rock, to as much as nine inches ; beneath this soil, the incisions are sharper and more distinct than those on the exposed surface. . . . .

"Some significancy seems to be involved in an eastward position ; for I find that the remans of Celtic dwellings, still to be seen on Beauly Moor, and on Hartside among the Cheviots, have their openings to the east. May there not be in this some indication— it may be faint—of the worship of the Sun, a fragment of eastern superstition, which regarded light, and the Sun, the greatest of all lights, as the type of the Good Spirit.

"Independently of their meaning, these relics cannot be viewed without interest, as the earliest examples of sculpture in our island. · I cannot regard them as the amusements of an idle soldiery, nor as plans of camps, the exercises of incipient engineers ; for their wide distribution, and notwithstanding differences in detail, their family resemblance, prove that they had a common origin, and indicate a symbolical meaning, representing some popular thought; and though I cannot spell the rude lettering, I fancy, since they are associated with the last remains of celtic heroes and sages, they tell of the faith and hope of the aboriginal inhabitants of Britain."

Nor has Mr. Tate had to hold this opinion altogether in solitude, for he says that Mr. Greenwell in 1863 adopted a similar view," It cannot, I think," he says, "be questioned, that their import is religious." We are reminded also that Sir Gardner Wilkinson in 1859, said, "I am not disposed to maintain the opinion which at first suggested itself to me, that they related to the circular camps, and certain dispositions connected with them." The camp fancy, says Mr. Tate, may therefore be abandoned ; indeed, the wonder is that it should ever have been entertained, for few indeed of the figures represent the arrangements of a camp ; both are more or less circular, but the resemblance ends there.

Strange indeed would it have been, if the people of the ancient period had from one end of the country to the other been employed in drawing entrenchments ; Dod Law, where they are so numerous, must have been the site of a military college. The square figures on the Dod Law stones, enclosing spaces covered over with cups, might help the fancy; but these are rare forms. The common figures do not represent any camp I have seen ; in camps, one, two, or three ramparts and ditches protect a large inner area ; but on stones where there are a number of inscribed concentric circles, the inner circle encloses only a small hollow ; four ramparts there are to a camp, but not more ; but some figures have eight circles."

Sir J. Simpson rejects in the most positive manner the astronomical theory, in which the cups and rings are supposed to be rude representations of the sun and stars, " nor," says he, " have we the slightest particle of evidence in favour of any of the numerous additional conjectures which have been proposed,—as that the British cup and ring carvings are symbolic enumerations of families or tribes ; or some variety of archaic writing ; or emblems of the philosophical views of the Druids ; or stone tables for Druidical sacrifices ; or objects for the practice of magic and necromancy."

Mr. Dickson of Alnwick, a friend of Sir J. Simpson's, speaking of the incised stones found upon the hills about Doddinton, Chatton, etc., suggested that these carvings relate to the god Mithras (the name under which the sun was worshipped in Persia) ; that about the end of the second century the religion of Mithras had extended over all the western empire, and was the favourite religion of the Romans, a system of astrological theology ; that in the sculptured Northumberland rocks, the central cup signifies the sun, the concentric circles, probably the orbits of the planets, and the radial straight groove, the way through to the sun. " In consequence," says Sir J. Simpson," " Mr. Dickson holds these rock sculptures to be the work of the Romans, and not Celtic, having been cut, he supposed, as emblems of their religion by Roman soldiers near old British camps, after they had driven out their native defenders. But if they were of Roman origin," adds Sir James, " they would surely be found in and around Roman stations, and not in old British localities—in Roman graves, and not in old British kistvaens. The fact, however, is that they abound in localities which no Roman soldiers ever occupied, as in Argyleshire, in Orkney, and in Ireland. And possibly even most of them were cut before the mythic time when Romulus drew his first encircling furrow around the Palatine Mount, and founded that pretty village which was destined to become—within seven or eight short centuries—the Empress of the civilized world.

"Some Archæologists have attempted to carry back the lapidary cuttings to the influence of an eastern race, who appear to have known the west, and perhaps the north, of Europe, for several centuries before Rome even was founded, and who are imagined to have cut the lapidary rings, not for the worship of the Persian god, Mithras, but of the Phœnician god, Baal."

Sir J. Simpson calls these cup and ring marks, "archæological enigmata, which we have no present power of solving; lapidary hieroglyphics and symbols, the key to whose mysterious import has been lost, and probably may never be regained."

The various explanations suggested by the Rev. Mr. Greenwell, Sir Gardner Wilkinson, Dr. Graves, and others, alluded to in these pages, he discards as altogether destitute of proof. The idea that they are archaic maps or plans of old circular camps and cities in their neighbourhood, he says, he believes has been abandoned as untenable by some, if not all, of the antiquaries who first suggested it. Nor does the suggestion that they were dials for marking time by the light of the sun find any favour with him, as they have been found in localities which neither sun nor shadow could reach, as in the dark interiors of stone sepulchres and underground houses. Nor that they were gambling tables, as they occur on perpendicular as well as flat rocks, and that they are used as covers for the ashes of the dead.

It has been suggested also, and by men of high attainments—archæologists and dignitaries of the Church—that the cups were emblems of old Lingam worship, but this explanation shares the same fate as the others, and Sir James calls it a supposition which appears to him to be totally without any anatomical or other foundation, and one altogether opposed to all we know of the specific class of symbols used in that worship, either in ancient or modern times.

"In Palestine and the country beyond Jordan, some of the marks found are so large that it has been supposed that they may have been used as small presses of wine, or as mortars for pounding the gleanings of wheat. But there is an objection to these theories as accounting for the marks generally, which is fatal to them. To serve these purposes, the rocks on which the marks occur, should be in a horizontal position, whereas in a majority of cases all over the world, these 'cups' are found either on shelving rocks, or on the sides of perpendicular stones. This renders worthless also the ideas which have at different times been put forward, that they may have been used for some sort of gambling game, or as sundials. A

Swiss archæologist who has lately devoted himself to the question, believes that he has recogonised in the sculpturings under his observation maps of the surrounding districts, the 'cups' indicating the mountain peaks. In the same way, others have thought that similar markings may have been intended as maps or plans, pointing out the direction and character of old circular camps and cities in their neighbourhood. But if any such resemblances have been discovered, they can hardly be other than fortuitous, since it is difficult to understand how rows of cup-marks, arranged at regular intervals, and in large numbers, could have served as representatives either of the natural features of a country, or of camps and cities. But a closer resemblance may be found in them as maps, if we suppose that they were intended to represent things in the heavens rather than on earth. The round cup-like marks are reasonably suggestive of the sun, moon, and stars, and if only an occasional figure could be found representing a constellation, some colour might be held to be given to the idea; but unfortunately this is not the case. Nevertheless, the shape of the marks has led many to believe that they are relics of the ancient sun worship of Phœnicia, and that their existence in Europe is due to the desire of the Phœnician colonists to convert our forefathers to their faith. But there are many reasons for regarding this theory, though supported by the authority of Professor Nilsson, as untenable. The observations of late years have brought to light cup-marks and megalithic circles in parts of Europe on which a Phœnician foot never trod; and it is a curious circumstance that in those portions of the British Isles most frequented by these indefatigable traders, there are fewer traces of these monuments than in the northern and inland districts, which were comparatively inaccessible to them. We know also that the early Phœnician travellers belonged to the bronze age, and we should therefore expect to find bronze implements in the tombs marked by cup sculpturings if these were carved either by the Phœnicians or their disciples. But, as a matter of fact, the only implements found are of wood, iron, and polished stone.

" But there is yet another reason for supposing that the cup-carvers belonged to a period far anterior to the arrival of the Phœnicians in Britain, and that is, that the markings have never been found in connection with any shape or form of letter-writing. This one fact in the face of the acknowledged tendency of people of every age and clime to inscribe characters and letters, when they possess a knowledge of any, on stones and rocks, is enough to prove that

G

these rock-carvers were ignorant of the use of letters. Thus people who accept the theory that the marks are, at any rate in some cases, artificial, are carried far back in the world's history, possibly to a time when dolicocephalic people, whose remains are found interred in long barrows, surrounded by stone implements, were the occupiers of the British Isles. But whoever these carvers were, and whenever they lived, it is beyond question that for considerable periods they must have inhabited almost every known country in the world, from China to Peru. And it is the difficulty of fixing the age in which they flourished, which gives to the identification of the marks shown to Fuh-he, its special interest. Here we have a date which enables us to trace back the existence of similar marks to the twenty-ninth century before Christ, or thereabouts. This, in conjunction with the general history of the sculpturings, still more completely disposes of the theories that they owe their origin to the sun worshipping Phœnicians, or to people of later times. As to their meaning, it will be seen from what has been said, that no satisfactory explanation of it has been offered ; and the Chinese legend, therefore, which states that an old man told the Emperor Yaou (B. C. 2356-2255) that they were records of the years of the Emperors, may fairly claim an equal hearing with the rest. It is further curious to observe that, while mention is made in the Chinese record of representations of vanda leaves having been found in conjunction with the marks, Mr. Fergusson points out that a palm leaf or fern occurs conjointed with cup-marks at New Grange in Ireland ; 'though how,' he remarks, 'a knowledge of an eastern plant reached New Grange, is by no means clear.'* This reference by Mr. Fergusson, with a diagram of the branch at New Grange, taken from a rubbing, will be found in his Rude Stone Monuments, p. 207.

    " The description given of the cup-marks by Mr. Rivett-Carnac, in the Journal of the Royal Asiatic Society of Bengal, suggested to M. Terrien de la Couperie, the idea that the " River Drawings," discovered by the Chinese Emperor, Fuh-he (B. C. 2852-2737), on the banks of the Ho, and upon which he is said to have founded the diagrams of the Book of Changes, were similar marks. A comparison between these as they have been handed down by tradition, and those described by Mr. Carnac, confirms the surmise.

    " The Chinese legend says, that on the occasion of Fuh-he's visit to the banks of the Ho, in the grass springing month, during the

* Sat. Rev., v. 56.

days when the rain descended, the Lungma brought drawings and presented them to him. These drawings, we are told, consisted of round starlike marks, arranged in rows; and that when forming from them his famous eight diagrams, he represented the rows, consisting of odd numbers, by straight unbroken lines, and those of even numbers by divided lines. As in all ancient legends, the story varies in the pages of different authors. Sometimes it is Hwang-te (B. c. 2697—2597), who, after having fasted for seven days, is presented on the banks of the Tui-kwei river, with drawings consisting of plain marks, vanda leaves, and red writings. At other times, it is Yaou (B. c. 2356—2255), who builds an altar at the junction of the Ho and Lo, and who has there laid before him a cuirass bearing inscriptions. But whether it be Fuh-he, Hwang-te, or Yaou, the marks are always described as having been brought to their notice on the banks of rivers, and generally in connection with altars or some sacred spots. Not only thus do the shape of markings, and form of the inscriptions agree with those observed by Mr. Rivett-Carnac, but the localities in which they occur are precisely similar. In Kumaun Valley, and elsewhere in India, the marks are invariably found in the neighbourhood of temples, of hillside altars, or of burial grounds. Those particularly described by Mr. Rivett-Carnac occur on a shelving rock, overhanging a stream near a temple of Mahadeo. In the small space of fourteen feet by twelve feet, there are no fewer than two hundred of these marks, arranged in lines, and in every possible combination. Among them also are examples of every known variety of the sculpturings. There are cup-marks, pure and simple, then again cup-marks surrounded by a ring or rings, and yet again others surrounded by a ring in a groove, forming together the shape of a jew's-harp. When questioned as to the origin of these sculpturings, the natives declared their belief that they were the work of either the giants of old, or of herdsmen, while others attributed them to the Pāndūs, an ancient people, who—like the Picts in Scotland and P'anku, in China—are supposed to have been the architects of every ancient monument in India which is without a recognised history. Mr. Rivett-Carnac throws out a suggestion that they may be the writings of a primitive race, and points out that the combinations in which they occur are sufficiently numerous to answer the requirements of writing." *

Mr. W. F. Wakeman says in the pages of the *Kilkenny Archæological Journal* :—" How is it that rock-carvings, of unknown, but

* Sat. Rev. v. 56.

remote antiquity, situate in various districts of the Old World, find
in South America their exact parallels ! After all, can it be that
tribes in a savage, or half barbarous state will, all over the globe,
and in every age, instinctively invent and adopt the same type of
symbol, the same style of decoration ? We well know how wonderfully similar are the carvings on the weapon handles, paddles,
etc., of the very recently expired (if indeed it do not yet struggle
for existence) 'Stone Age' in New Zealand, to the ornamentation
found on the majority of our sepulchral urns, and many other objects of the period of cremation, in the north and west of Europe.
The warriors and chiefs of New Zealand tatooed their persons with
fanciful, or perhaps, symbolic figures, spirals, chevrons, circles, etc.,
as many embalmed human heads, still well preserved in museums,
testify.   Their implements and arms were similarly ornamented.
This work was performed during *their* 'Stone Age.'   Our civilized
ancestors are recorded to have painted their bodies during what, as
far as can be made out, appears to have been the close of our ' Age
of Stone.'   In more ways than one, the art ideas of the British
Islander, of upwards of two thousand years ago, and those of the
modern Maori, appear to have been almost identical.   How far into
the past such styles of decorating and engraving extended, no man
can say.   We know when they decayed in New Zealand.   In Ireland, it would seem that the practice of rock-marking, properly so
called, ended with the period of cremation ; and it is well worthy of
noting,as Joyce has remarked in words somewhat equivalent to these
' That neither in the traditions of the people, nor in our earliest
manuscripts which treat of Pagan times and usages, can be found
the slightest reference to the practice of cremation and urn
burial."

How long then, anterior to the advent of St. Patrick, must that
custom have been in disuse !   The Scoti are famous for long
memories.   All our Pagan historical characters, of whose obsequies
we know anything, have been buried, not burnt ; all our cromlechs,
or dolmens, as a rule, yield calcined human bones, and cinerary
urns which often contain implements of flint and bone, of truly
primitive type."

Speaking of the markings on the rocks of certain parts of Ireland,
Dean Graves says :—" It may readily be imagined that the inscriptions here described have given rise to many speculations as to
their nature.   It was to be presumed that the persons who carved
the inscriptions intended to represent circular objects of some kind
or other.   But what could these objects have been ?   Some have

suggested shields. This notion seems inconsistent with the fact that the same stone presents so many circular symbols of different sizes, varying from the small shallow cup of an inch or two in diameter, to the group of concentric circles two feet across. It also seems probable that, as shields in general used to bear distinctive devices, these would re-appear in the inscriptions ; but the inscribed circles exhibit no such variety as might have been expected on this hypothesis. Again, if the circles represented shields, what could be meant by the openings in the circumference of many of them. Lastly, what connexion could there be between the idea of shields, and the long lines appearing in the Staigue monument, or the short ones on that at Ballynasare.

"Another idea was, that these figures were designed to represent astronomical phenomena. This notion was perhaps the most obvious, and the least easily disproved. It harmonizes also with what has been handed down respecting the elemental worship of the Pagan Celts. Nevertheless, it seems open to obvious objections. In astronomical diagrams, one could hardly fail to recognise a single symbol conspicuous amongst the rest as denoting the sun or moon, or two such symbols denoting both these bodies. One might also expect to see some delineation, even by the rudest hand, of the phases of the moon. We look in vain for these indications of an astronomical reference in the groups of lines and circles figured. Again, this supposition fails to account for the openings in the circles, and the lines which appear in connexion with them.

" A countryman at Staigue bridge suggested that these circles were intended to serve as moulds, in which metal rings might be cast. This explanation is decisively negatived by the fact that the circles occur on parts of rocks which are not horizontal.

" Another proposed idea was that the circles were used for the purpose of playing some game. The great dissimilarity which exists between the figures on the different stones renders this explanation improbable.

" The idea which occurred to my own mind was, that the incised circles were intended to represent the circular buildings of earth or stone, of which the traces still exist in every part of Ireland. The conjecture is supported by the following considerations :—

" 1. The circles are of different sizes, and some are disposed in concentric groups. The ancient dwellings and fortified seats of the ancient Irish were circular ; they were of various sizes, from the small cloghan, or stone house of ten feet in diameter, to the great camp including an area of some acres ; and the principal forts had several concentric *valla*.

" 2. The openings in the inscribed circles may have been intended to denote the entrances.

" 3. The other inscribed lines may have represented roads passing by or leading up to the forts.

" The conjecture that these carvings were primitive maps, representing the disposition of the neighbouring forts, appeared to be a fanciful one ; and discouraged by the scepticism of the friends to whom I communicated it, I laid aside the drawings and rubbings for some years, hoping that some light might be thrown upon the subject, by the discovery of monuments, the purpose of which was more evident.

" This expectation has not been fulfilled. Nevertheless, I have some hope, that my original guess has been confirmed in such a way as to warrant me in submitting it for the judgment of our antiquaries.

" In the course of last autumn, after a careful examination of the drawings, I came to the conclusion that the centres of the circles, and the neighbouring cups and dots, arrange themselves generally three by three in straight lines. This disposition of the symbols could not be said to be perfectly accurate; but I thought I could observe close and designed approximation to it. If then the circles represent forts, and are disposed three by three in straight lines on the inscribed stones, I saw that we might expect to find the forts disposed in like manner over the surface of the country ; and I think that I have succeeded in verifying this inference. The ancient raths have fortunately been laid down on the six-inch Ordnance Survey Maps of Ireland ; and, unless I am deceived by fortuitous collineations, I find that the forts are actually arranged three by three in straight lines. The discovery of this fact, if it be a fact, would be of much more consequence than the explanation of the meaning of the inscriptions of which I have given an account. But this further inquiry must be conducted with care. Large portions of the country must be examined, and those difficulties must be confronted which the disappearance of ancient remains must inevitably give rise to."

It is considered by antiquarians that the wide distribution of cup and ring marks over the British Islands, " not only from the far north in Orkney, to the south in Devonshire, but also into Ireland, evidences, that at the period when they were made, the whole of Britain was peopled by tribes of one race, who were imbued with

with the same superstitions, and expressed them by the same symbols."

" The opinion has been maintained that these sculptures were the work of Roman soldiers, who, after driving the native population out of their camps, occupied them, and caused the emblems of their own religion, relating to Mithraic rites, to be carved on the rocks in the district around. But such rude incisions possess none of the characters of Roman workmanship; nor have Roman relics of any kind ever been found in connection with them. The fancy, however, is completely refuted by the fact that these sculptures occur in districts—as in Ireland, and in the Orkneys—which were never trodden by the foot of the Roman conquerors.

" The invariable association of these inscriptions with ancient British forts, oppida, villages, and sepulchres, is evidence of all having been the work of the people who dwelt in those villages, and were buried in those tombs. The proof has been cumulative; and it amounts to a demonstration when we observe at Ford West Field, at Black Heddon, at Craigie Hill, at Lochgilphead, and at Kerry, typical symbols, inscribed on the covers and side stones of ancient British cists; for these sculptures could not have been of later age than the interments; they may have been earlier, as they might have been quarried from a sacred inscribed stone in the neighbourhood, and placed over or in the cist to give a sanctity to the resting place of the dead. These inscriptions, therefore, are pre-Roman, and many date backwards not less than two thousand years, and I am inclined to believe some five hundred or a thousand years more; because the relics of the period indicate a low degree of civilization, and would carry us back to the early immigration of Celts into Britain.

" I have applied the general phrase ancient British to this period; and avoided using terms more definite, because the question has been raised, whether our forts, dwellings, sepulchres, and inscriptions are referable to the Celts, the race who peopled Britain when Cæsar made his descent on the island; or to a prior race—a race of feebler organization and lower civilization still, who had been driven away or exterminated by an irruption of Celts. The determination of the question is not without some difficulty, arising chiefly from the results of recent investigations into the ethnology of the people who were buried long ages ago in the little stone chests found in the district, covered with heaps of stones and earth. The first cranium critically examined and described, was found in a cist at Tosson, near Rothbury, along with urns, cannel-coal orna-

ments, bronze buckles, and an iron weapon ; and this proved to be
the broad short form called Brachy-cephalic. Since that time, some
dozen other crania have been found and examined, all obtained
within the area of the ancient province of the Otadeni—from Ilder-
ton, North Sunderland, Alnwick, Grindstone Law, in Northumberland ; and from near Dunse and Cockburnspath, in Berwickshire ;
and all these crania were of the same type as that from Tosson.
This shape of skull, however, is not supposed to correspond with
that of the modern Celts—of the Irish, Welsh, or Gaels,—which is
represented to be closely allied to that of the English and other
nations belonging to the great Aryan family, whose skulls are of
the Dolicho-cephalic type, or long oval form.

"Retzius, and other Scandinavian ethnologists refer the Brachy-
cephalic crania to men of the stone age, whose descendants now
live in the inhospitable regions of Lapland ; and Dr. Wilson, in
his last edition of his " Pre-Historic Annals," has adopted the hypothesis of there having been in Britain two pre-Celtic races ; and
strangely enough, he has placed the Tosson skull among the stone
age and bronze age men, ignoring the fact that it was associated
with an iron weapon.

There is a strong tendency at present to lengthen out the age of
our old antiquities : against this we must guard, especially when
it is connected with refined theorising which would distort facts to
suit artificial classifications. Ethnology alone, however, cannot
yet be taken as an authoritative guide ; the data are not yet sufficiently exact and numerous to enable any one to dogmatise as to
the typical form of the modern Celtic skull. Before drawing a conclusion, we must gather additional information from other lines of
research. Language gives important evidence ; for the old names
of hills, ruins, and other prominent objects—names given by the
aboriginal inhabitants, which oftentimes survive the revolutions of
race—are Celtic. Chalmers in his " Caledonia," has with great
ability and research proved this. The era of one ancient British
Oppidum, similar to Greaves Ash, has been linked with the Celtic
race ; for in Carn Brae, in Cornwall, coins of the Celtic Kings of
Britain have been found ; proving that such forts have been in use
at the time of the Roman invasion, though their original construction may have been earlier by many centuries.

"A people so numerous as the Celts were, when Cæsar invaded
Britain—he calls them an infinite multitude—would surely leave
some traces of their occupancy of the island ; but if the forts, oppida, barrows, and stone circles, which we have in Northumberland,

are not their remains, it may be asked, where are they to be found?
For if we attribute these remains to an earlier race, we would blot
out the records of many centuries from our annals. Taking therefore, into account various kinds of evidence, we may conclude that
the old remains in Northumberland, our sculptures included, belong to the Celtic race, though they may tell the history of many
centuries prior to the Christian era. The apparent discrepancy of
ethnology with this conclusion is suggestive of further inquiry.
May not the type of cranium have gradually changed through long
ages of advancing civilization? Or may not the effect have been
produced even by a slight admixture of a new and dominating
race." *

"The question may well be asked," says Sir William Wilde,
" what was the purpose of those markings; are they mere ornamental carvings, or are they inscriptions from which the history of
this monument, or whatever it was originally intended for, might
be learned? Are they ideographical, or hierographic, in the strict
sense of that word; that is, sacred carving? To this latter we are
inclined; and if we may be allowed to coin a word to express our
meaning, we would call them Tymboglyphics, or tomb writing, for
similar characters have as yet only been found connected with the
vestiges of ancient sepulchres, as here, at Dowth, and on tombs of
a like character in the counties of Down and Donegal. That the
meaning of these scriptures, if any such they have, beyond being
sacred to the dead, shall ever be brought to light from the haze of
obscurity which now enshrouds them, is very problematical."

The Rev. James Greaves in his communication to the Kilkenny
Archæological Journal, in July, 1865, reminded his readers that
many of the markings of New Grange and Dowth had been proved
to have been carved before the stones were used for their present
purpose, and he draws from that fact this inference:—"If we find
carvings on a natural boulder of unwrought stone, not in any way
connected with a Christian use, or a Christian tradition, and not
ostensibly intended to be used in any structure, although these
carvings may not be strictly analogous to those at New Grange,
Dowth, or Sileve-na-caillighe, yet we have some grounds to conclude
that here is an example of a primæval custom which placed ready
to the hand of the builders of these tumuli, materials ready carved,
and possibly endowed with some kind of sanctity fitting them to
do honour to a great chieftain's grave."

Tate's Ancient Sculptured Rocks.

Mr. Graves is here referring to a natural boulder of arenaceous limestone, one of a number found in King's County, in the locality of the Seven Churches of Clonmacnoise. "On both sides of the Shannon in this neighbourhood," he says, "Christian tradition is busy with almost every stone, boher, and tougher, and close to this boulder, on the old boher which led to the Seven Churches of Clonmacnoise before the present road was formed, is a cairn called Leacht-na-Marra, or the Monument of the Dead, where to the present day, when a funeral approaches that famed burial ground, the coffin is laid down, and stones thrown on the carn. But I was distinctly informed that no Christian rite was ever performed at the Clonfinlough stone : on the contrary, the name by which it is known—'The Fairy's Stone'—points to a Pagan origin. Another legend terms it 'The Horseman's Stone,' and tells that a horseman gallops round it at certain times."

The Clonfinlough boulder presents a flat surface, and is of irregular form ; its extreme measurements being 9 feet 9 inches, by 8 feet 3 inches ; it slopes to the south, and at the western side the sward had grown over a portion of it. The other boulders occuring on the osker are studded over with cup-like hollows, evidently caused by the solvent property of rain water, retained in certain natural irregularities, which were thereby deepened, and assumed the artificial aspect which they now present. The drawing made by my friend, Mr. G. V. Du Noyer, gives an excellent idea of the carvings which cover the entire of the surface of the "Fairy's Stone," and one cannot escape the impression, that many of the cup-like hollows which enter into the several groups of carvings were the natural results of the lodgement of rain-water, perhaps deepened, and in some cases, others added to complete the figures ; as for instance, two resembling a sun with its attendant planets, and another bearing a striking likeness to the constellation of the Plough. In other cases these hollows have been connected by incised lines in the form of crosses ; or taken advantage of to indicate the pommels of rudely marked daggers; or they have been elongated, and by the connexion of two of them, made to resemble the impressions of the human foot, of which several occur on the stone. But the most singular markings on the boulder are representations of the ancient Irish ring-brooch ; some with a knob on the top of the acus, as frequently occurs in extant specimens; others being flat at top, and seeming to represent the looping of the acus over the flat bar of an half-moon ring. It only remains for me to add, that the carvings appear to have been formed by a rude pointed tool or pick, and are on an average about an inch deep. I am not myself aware of the existence of any other example analogous to the Clonfinlough stone; but Mr. Cooke has sent me a sketch of an incised stone near Cranna, co. Galway, called by the peasantry, the ' stone of the fruitful fairy.' This fairy stone is a boulder of very irregular form, measuring 46 in. by 32 in.; it presents the water-worn hollows already described, but they are of a larger size; also one or two well marked dagger-like figures, and crosses. There are also V-shaped markings, but no foot-marks or ring-brooch carvings."

Sir J. Simpson endeavours to impress upon his readers the fact that all the cup-like excavations which we meet with on megalithic circles, monoliths, etc., are not by any means the work of man. Many of them, he declares, are on the contrary, the work of nature; or in other words, the result of the weathering and disintegration of the stone from long exposure. He says : " Among the endless vagaries of shape and form effected on rocks by weathering, cup-like excavations occur frequently on the surfaces of primary sandstone and other softer rocks, like those of the Lundie Stones in Fife, and the Duddo Circle in Northumberland; and I have found them also on the surfaces of far denser stones. Occasionally they are the result of the mineralogical constitution of the rock, as of softer portions weathering out, or of the enucleation of fossilized organic remains, or of embedded stone nodules. Thus the surface of the Carline Stone, near Dunmore House, presents a series of smooth cup-like excavations; but they are all the result of round included masses having been weathered out of the amygdaloid rock of which the stone is composed. Nor are all cup-like excavations, which are not the effect of weathering, the result of human agency. On visiting the so-called cromlech or chambered tumulus on the Orme's Head above Llandudno, I found various excavations on its stones, and especially on the interior of the covering stone; but a little examination of their smooth surfaces and expanding interiors showed that the excavations had been the work of the Pholas, when these stones formed part of the sea-beach.

"In many cases it is difficult, and indeed impossible, to determine conclusively whether cup-excavations, when found alone, are the product of human art, or the product of nature. But various collateral circumstances often tend to evince their artificial origin, such as—(1) The limited size, regular rounded forms, smooth surfaces, and shallow depths of the excavations; (2) Their existence upon the surfaces of rocks too hard to be readily weathered; (3) Their arrangements in rows, or in other artificial positions and groupings not referable to any mineralogical peculiarities in the stone; and (4), and specially, their co-existence with other cups, surrounded by single or multiple rings."

In a footnote appended to the above, we read :—" The very hard 'Sarsen' stones, or tertiary sandstone grits of Abury and Stonehenge show in many parts weathered irregular cavities and excavations; some of them large and deep. Speaking of the Abury stone, Dr. Stukeley long ago observed, ' In some places I thrust my cane, a yard long, up to the handle, in holes and cavities worked through by age, which (he argues) must needs bespeak some thousands of years continuance.' (*See his Abury, pp. 17 and 39.*) The massive rusty conglomerate blocks, forming the circles at Stanton Drew are still more remarkably drilled with crystalline cavities, and the corrosions of time."

Discussing the question of the origin and meaning of the cup and ring marks, Mr. Allen says that had these hieroglyphics existed in Egypt or Persia, or China, or in fact, any other country but our own, we should have long ago filled our museums with casts of them, and have left no stone unturned until their meaning was fully deciphered. They have, however, the misfortune to be found close to our own doors, and are therefore treated with that contempt which anything that does not appertain to classical learning seems to meet with in England. The only representatives of this class of prehistoric sculpture in the British Museum are two miserable little fragments at the top of one of the cases.

" The state of our knowledge may be briefly summed up as follows : (1) As to their geographical distribution. Stones with cup and ring markings are found widely scattered over the whole of the British Isles, also in various parts of France, Germany, Switzerland, Denmark, Sweden, and Norway. (2) As to the classes of monuments on which they are found. These are as follow :—Natural rock surfaces—Isolated boulders—Near ancient British fortified towns and camps—In connection with lake dwellings, underground houses, and Pictish towers—On single standing stones—On groups of standing stones—On stone circles—On cromlechs—In chambered cairns—On cist covers—On urn covers—On grave-stones in Christian churchyards—On the walls of churches themselves.

" From the fact of cup markings being found in so many instances directly associated with sepulchral remains, I think it may fairly be inferred that they are connected in some way or other with funeral rites, either as sacred emblems or for actual use in holding small offerings or libations. I am aware, however, that the fact of their being found occasionally on vertical surfaces is rather against the latter assumption. The connecting grooves are suggestive of channels for carrying off liquids.

"After seeing several hundred of these stones in England and Scotland, I have been forcibly struck by two points : (1) the absence of any definite arrangement of any kind in the position of the cups; and (2) the continual recurrence of the same monotonous figures of cups, rings, and grooves, repeated hundreds of times with hardly any variation of any kind, or tendency to develope into more ornamental forms. The absence of appearance of design in the arrangement of the cups might be accounted for by supposing that they were executed one by one, at different times, either by the same or different individuals. With regard to no advance being made beyond the cup, ring, and groove, I think it points to what was before suggested, _i.e._, that they were either a well recognised symbol frequently repeated, or that the shape of the cup, ring, and groove, adapted itself specially to some ceremonial use.

The method of execution of the carving appears to have been by punching with a pointed instrument, the tool marks being in many instances very distinct where the stone has been protected by earth above it, either in a cairn or otherwise. The circles are not struck from a centre, and are often irregular.

Finally, with regard to the age of the sculptures, it is attested, (1) by the very large area over which they are scattered ; (2) the absence of any traditions as to their meaning ; (3) their being found as covers to urns, inside cairns belonging to the late stone or early bronze age.

Their use has survived down to a comparatively recent period, as they have been found near Inverness, by Mr. Jolly, on gravestones in Christian churchyards ; and also they have been noticed on the walls of brick churches in Germany. In some cases they are still anointed with grease as a superstitious ceremony. Where the carvings occur on rock surfaces, it is almost always in special isolated districts, which may have been considered sacred in ancient times. In Scotland, France, Switzerland, and Germany, cups alone are found as a general rule, whereas, in England, Ireland, and Sweden, rings and grooves are almost always associated with the cups. In Sweden, figures of men and boats are also added." *

"Cup and ring marks have never been as yet found in connection with inscriptions of any kind, and may therefore be considered

---

* Journal Arch. Assoc., 38.

as pre-historic. Beyond this and the fact of their being found on cromlechs, menhirs, megalithic circles, and other remains of the same period, nothing is at present known which finally determines their age ; but that it is very considerable, may be gathered from the large area over which these sculptures are found to be distributed. Professor Nilsson refers these sculptures to the bronze-age." *

"Cup and ring marks have been said to be intended for rude representations of objects of every-day use, such as circular shields, annular brooches, etc. Some think that they were burial tablets for the common people, who could not afford to have a megalithic circle erected to their memory. Others think they were used as gambling tables ; but it must be remembered that the marks occur on the vertical and sloping faces of rocks, and also in exposed situations, and again, on the cover stones of burial urns." †

"Some think that the groups of cup and ring marks are maps of the stars, but as far as I am aware, no arrangement of cups has ever been identified with either any well known constellation." ‡

"The late Professor O'Curry was strongly of opinion that a portion of the people of Erin, even in days many centuries antecedent to the birth of Christ, possessed some method of recording events, etc., etc., other than by oral communication. However this may be, we can hardly imagine any lengthy historical record being embodied in work like that we are now referring to. It is very curious to observe how various and far separated are the districts, even climates, in which this style of rock and other carving prevailed. The general design is every where nearly the same, and would on slight consideration appear to have been produced by one race. Such, however, cannot be the case. It may surprise not a few of the readers of this paper, as I confess it did myself, to learn that in several portions of South America, especially in the districts of Northern Bolivia, at Ribeirao, are rock inscriptions, which, if found upon an Irish monument of the New Grange, or Knockmany class, would not be considered as presenting any new variety of our archaic scorings. These inscriptions are stated to be cut into the hardest rock, and from their corroded appearance to show traces of a very remote age."

Reference is here made to a discovery made by an American engineering expedition in the year 1853, of these rocks at Ribeirao.

---

* Journal Arch. Assoc., 35, p. 25.

† ‡ Journ. Arch. Assoc., 35, p. 24.

The expedition reached the first rapid of the Amazon, San Antonio, on the 16th July. Here they found it necessary to unload their canoes, and transport all the cargoes overland for a distance of over a quarter of a mile, on the left margin of the river. While accompanying the boatmen who were engaged in this task, they discovered upon different granite ledges, some very curious marks crossing each other at various angles, and cut into the rock to a depth of one hundredth part of a meter. They afterwards found more numerous marks of the same kind at the 'rapid of Teotonio, and just above; but it was at the rapid of Ribeirao, that the most extraordinary of these tracings was found. Here they were cut into the hardest rock, and appeared like letters, which, from their corroded surfaces, showed traces of very great age. To translate from the M. M. Keller's report to the Government of Brazil :—" The great and patient labour which was necessary to cut these signs in stone of this nature, without any iron tools, and only by erosion with another stone, leads us to the belief that they are not the labour of indolence, and that they have some signification, especially those of Ribeirao. The latter form an interesting parallel with the rough representations of celestial objects and of animals, upon the rocks of the Orinoco, described by Humboldt."

The American markings consist chiefly of concentric circles, with or without the central dot, or cup; spirals, semi-circles of concentric lines; oghamic-looking strokes; "spectacle" forms; and, strange to say, of simple and compound crosses, such as are to be seen in several of our megalithic chambers, and sometimes, in various parts of Ireland, upon the surface of the " earth-fast" rock, as at Aughaglach, co. Fermanagh; Ryefield, co. Cavan, or on the walls of natural caverns, as at Knockmore, co. Fermanagh, and Loughnacloyduff in the same territory.*

The theory that cup and ring marks were religious symbols, Mr. Allen regards as among the most probable suggestions, " since they are continually found associated with burial rites, being carved on the stones of sepulchral circles and chambers, and on the cover stones of cinerary urns. Professor Nilsson believes that they are connected with Baal and sun worship. In support of this a few facts may be mentioned. Cup marks exist on a granite block, known as Balder's Stone, near Falkoping, in Sweden. The name Baal occurs continually in the north of England and in Scotland; for instance, in Yorkshire, Balderston, Baal's Hills; in Scotland,

* Kilkenny Arch. Jourl., 1879.

east coast, Bell's Hill, festival of Beltane, etc. The symbol for the sun, used by the Chinese, and also by other nations, is a circle with a dot in the centre, in later times a square with a dash through it. The Greek letter Θ is the nearest approach to this amongst the alphabets of the Western world, and it may be mentioned that it means a serpent."

One mode of accounting for these cups and rings is that they owe their origin to natural causes, such as the mechanical action of water, and the disintegrating power of storm, wind, and rain. However true this may be in some cases, it will certainly not account for the obviously artificial grouping and symmetrical shape, says Mr. Allen, not referable to the lithological composition of the stone. "As an example of a rock basin of clearly human production, that at Rath Michael (co. Dublin), may be mentioned. It is of exceedingly regular shape, and cut deep into hard quartzose rock, which has no tendency to weather in this manner. The co-existence of rock basins and cups with concentric rings and grooves makes their artificial character tolerably certain.

The theory has been started and held in some quarters, that cup and ring marks owe their origin to mere acts of caprice and idleness on the part of the prehistoric savage, that he had no intention of doing anything in particular when he excavated or drew them. But, as it has often been pointed out, this certainly will not explain the constant repetition of the same forms of markings throughout the whole of Great Britain, and in many other parts of the world. Still further, many of these sculpturings are made in the hardest rocks, and in most inconvenient and well-nigh inaccessible positions; with the rough tools known to primitive ages, it is scarcely likely that from sheer idleness men would undertake labour so wearying and difficult.

The suggestion that " ornamentation " is the key to the mystery, sounds rather odd perhaps, and one very unlikely to come from men of intellectual ability ; it, nevertheless, has been made, and by scholars of no mean authority. But, supposing this to be a satisfactory explanation of the markings as found on ancient mausolea, on the great curb-stone at the entrance of New Grange, or in the granite blocks forming the props of the passage into the sepulchral chamber at Gavr Inis, it seems impossible to apply it with any degree of probability to those wild and rugged masses of rock found in remote parts of various countries, far away from the habitations of men, and seldom looked upon save by the sunlight or the passing bird.

The elaborately sculptured stones and crosses of Scotland and Ireland, decorated by endless and elegant scrolls, circles, volutes, chevrons, and other interlaced and ever varying patterns cut upon their faces and sides, cited by C. J. Simpson as evidence of the ornamentation theory, are nothing whatever to the point, and cannot possibly throw any light upon the roughly cut cup, or ring, or channel found on the mountain side, or upon a sandstone rock possessing no other form than that given to it by nature.

Theorise as we may about these markings, it is tolerably evident that without further revelation or discovery, it is impossible to offer any explanation relative to their origin which shall be conclusive enough to carry conviction to the mind that the real solution has been reached. Speculation has been freely indulged in from the hour of their discovery, but the mystery is as deep as ever, and unless fuller information be forthcoming, will probably remain so. Probably, however, Mr. Tate is right, when in summing up the evidence for the different views propounded, he says, "additional facts observed confirm the conclusions reached some time ago, first, that these inscriptions have been made by the Celtic race occupying Britain many centuries before the Christian era; and second, that the figures are symbolical—most probably of religious ideas. Look at the extent of their distribution, from one extremity of Britain to the other, and even into Ireland; and say, what could induce tribes, being hundreds of miles apart, and even separated by the sea, to use precisely the same symbols, save to express some religious sentiments, or to aid in the performance of some superstitious rites."

Without dogmatising upon the matter, we may say that we, too, find it almost impossible to avoid some such conclusion, and after long and close study of the ancient religions of the eastern and western worlds, we feel that the phallic explanation is that which has the greatest claim to our consideration. Let any one inspect the plates in works delineating the Hindu Pantheon, and compare the drawings of the lingam-yoni with many of the rock markings we have described—with those for instance on the frontispiece of this book—and they will find it difficult to avoid the conclusion that there is a manifest and striking connection. The fact is, the phallic idea has prevailed all over the world to a far greater extent than many have ever imagined, and superficial observers have passed by many things as inexplicable which came properly within its domain, and which thus recognised, would have been readily understood. It is not, of course, to the gross forms of the Priapus used in ancient Greek, Roman, or Egyptian festivals, that we allude, but to the much more refined, and, if we may so call it, modest lingam worship of India. What was the image—the lingam-yoni —which stood in the temple, and before which the worshipper bent in adoration, and to which was brought the various offerings prescribed in the sacred books? Speaking generally, it was formed of stone, and consisted of a base three or four feet high, the top of which was surrounded with a raised rim; in the middle it was slightly excavated, and raised on a level with the rim, the figure of a yoni (pudendum muliebre), from the centre of which rose a smooth round stone slightly conical towards the top, of a foot and a half in height, and about three inches diameter at the base. If this be compared with some, at any rate, of the rock markings, a very distinct resemblance at once suggests itself. Even Sir J. Simpson feels constrained to admit that the position and circumstances in which they were placed, rendered it extremely probable that they were in some way connected with the religious thoughts of those who carved them, the question is, how—in what manner? The phallic explanation, really comes in quite naturally when we consider the vast extent to which that form of worship prevailed, and the disposition of men everywhere to represent in the sculptured form, the organs, male and female, to which they rendered obeisance. It seemed that what they adored, they must look upon, and the sense of propriety which in some quarters made it improper to come into personal contact with, or even to gaze at, the actual and living physical form, regarded with profound complacency and approbation the symbolical representation. Very much veiled, that symbolism was, sometimes, so much so, indeed, that even in India—its special and peculiar home—its form to the uninitiated was frequently unrecognisable. Yet in that land with numerous and magnificent temples, and abundance of wealth to procure all that luxury and imagination could desire, the object of worship was sculptured in comparatively remarkable resemblance to its human original. Very different would it necessarily be amongst less cultivated people, worshippers of the same object, with perhaps few or no temples, and only the very crudest ideas of art, and the most limited choice of material. Under such altered circumstances, they would have to be content with mere scratchings or coloured drawings on the rocks, of the rudest and most incomplete character—intelligible enough to the men who made them, and those for whom they were made, but mysterious and unmeaning to all not in the secret, and still more mysterious to the people of future ages, to whom the particular form of worship in question was utterly unknown.

Accepting, then, the concessions made by certain writers, just alluded to, that many of the archaic markings we have described, bore most probably a religious character, we advance a step further and suggest, in addition, that most probably that religion was phallic—the worship of the creative and regenerative forces of nature, and that the circles and incisions, the cups and channels, and some other similar sculpturings, actually often represented, though in a vague and half concealed way, the distinguishing features and marks of the two sexes of living beings. This may be regarded by some as simply a theory, and popular and deeply-rooted prejudice may reject it without proper consideration, but we submit it with confidence to the attention of those who have given any amount of study to the subject of nature or sex-worship, as the probable solution of much that has long been regarded as too mystical ever to be understood. Let a little more attention be paid to that worship, and in connection therewith let the character of the rock markings be duly considered, and probably the connection will become apparent, or at least, appear likely.

THE END.

Nature Worship and Mystical Series,

Cr. 8vo, Vellum, 7s. 6d. each.

Only a very limited number, PRIVATELY PRINTED.

———

PHALLICISM.—A Description of the Worship of **Lingam-Yoni** in various parts of the World, and in different Ages, with an Account of Ancient and Modern Crosses, particularly of the **Crux Ansata** (or Handled Cross) and other Symbols connected with the Mysteries of **Sex Worship.** (*Only in sets*).

OPHIOLATREIA.—An Account of the Rites and Mysteries connected with the Origin, Rise, and Development of **Serpent Worship** in various parts of the World, enriched with Interesting Traditions, and a full description of the celebrated Serpent Mounds and Temples, the whole forming an exposition of one of the phases of **Phallic,** or **Sex Worship.**

PHALLIC OBJECTS, MONUMENTS AND REMAINS; Illustrations of the Rise and Development of the **Phallic Idea** (Sex Worship), and its embodiment in Works of Nature and Art. *Etched Frontispiece.*

CULTUS ARBORUM.—A Descriptive Account of **Phallic Tree Worship,** with illustrative Legends, Superstitious Usages, etc. ; exhibiting its Origin and Development amongst the Eastern and Western Nations of the World, from the earliest to modern times.

This work has a valuable bibliography which will be of the greatest use and value to the student of Ancient Faiths. It contains references to nearly five hundred works on Phallism and kindred subjects.

Nature Worship and Mystical Series.—*cont.*

FISHES, FLOWERS, AND FIRE as ELEMENTS AND DEITIES in the **Phallic Faiths and Worship** of the Ancient Religions of GREECE, BABYLON, ROME, INDIA, etc., with illustrative Myths and Legends.

ARCHAIC ROCK INSCRIPTIONS; an Account of the Cup and Ring Marking on the Sculptural Stones of the Old and New Worlds. *With etched frontispiece.*

This subject, though comparatively a new one, and upon which a very limited amount of literature has been written, has excited considerable curiosity among its discoverers. These strange figures and marks bear the same resemblance whether found in England, Ireland, Scotland, India, Mexico, Brazil, North America, Sweden, etc. Probably the cup and ring markings were connected with the religious mysteries surrounding the worship of Baal. They are asserted on good authority to be Phallic Symbols, which subject the author has treated of in the present work.

NATURE WORSHIP, or an Account of **Phallic Faiths** and Practices, Ancient and Modern, including the Adoration of the Male and Female Powers, and the SACTI PUJA of INDIAN GNOSTICISM, by the author of Phallicism.

MYSTERIES OF THE ROSIE CROSS, or the History of that Curious Sect of the Middle Ages, known as the ROSICRUCIANS, with Examples of their Pretensions and Claims.

BIBLIOTHECA MADRIGALIANA.—A Bibliographical Account of Musical and Political Works published in England during the Sixteenth and Seventeenth Centuries, under the titles of Madrigals, Ballets, Ayres, Canzonets, etc., by Edward F. Rimbault, LL.D., F.S.A., 8vo, *cloth.* 2s. 6d.

BANBURY CHAP-BOOKS, and Nursery Toy Book Literature of the XVIII. and Early XIX. Centuries, *with impressions from several hundred original woodcut blocks by T. & J. Bewick, Blake, Cruikshank, Craig, Lee, Austin, and others,* Illustrating Favourite Nursery Classics, with their Antiquarian, Historical, Literary, and Artistic Associations, faithfully gleaned from the Original Works, with very much that is interesting and valuable appertaining to the early Typography and Topography of Children's Books relating to Great Britain and America, by Edwin Pearson. Cr. 4to. Paper boards. 6s. 1890

" Under a title long enough to stand beside that of Nares's 'Life of Burleigh,' Mr. Reader has issued, in a limited edition, a large series of the chap-book and nursery-book illustrations which remained in vogue till near the middle of the century. Very unequal in merit are these, extending from the most rudely executed wood-blocks of primitive times, to the works of Bewick and Cruikshank. They are, however, of equal interest. Mr. Pearson has not confined himself to the Banbury Press, but has dealt with other presses at York, Newcastle, Bath, and elsewhere. The first series of cuts he gives are those by John Bewick, executed for the ' Surprising Adventures of Phillip Quarll.' All but inexhaustible is, however, the matter, including various sets of illustrations to Æsop's ' Fables,' 'Jack the Giant Killer,' ' Goody Two Shoes,' ' Blue Beard,' &c. These are carefully reproduced. ' Banbury Chap-Books ' is both entertaining and valuable. It will commend the volume to book lovers to say that it is likely in time to become as scarce as are the books and leaflets which it reproduces."—NOTES AND QUERIES.

JORDAN.—Public and Private Life of that Celebrated Actress, MRS. JORDAN, late Mistress of George IV., Delineating the Vicissitudes of her Early Life, the Splendour of of her Noontide Blaze, as Mistress of the King, and Numerous Anecdotes of Illustrious and Fashionable Characters of the Day. Cr. 8vo. Parchment. 3s. 6d.

J. Duncombe

This work contains numerous anecdotes and statements not to be found in Boaden's Life of Mrs. Jordan. Boaden took rather a one sided view in favour of Royalty, while the present work exposes the cruel way she was treated by her Royal Protector, with an interesting account of her forcible detention at St. Cloud, where she died broken hearted.

MATRIMONIAL CEREMONIES DISPLAYED.

—Wherein are exhibited the various Customs, Odd Pranks, Whimsical Tricks and Surprising Practises of near one hundred diffcrent Kingdoms and Peoples in the World, now used in the Celebration and Consummation of Matrimony, collected from the Papers of a **Rambling Batchelor**, with the Adventures of Sir Harry Fitzgerald and his **Seven Wives**. Cr. 8vo, Japanese parchment, 6s.

The above volume describes the extensive and extraordinary ceremonies of the different nations of the world, including an interesting account of the more free and easy rites of the savage tribes. There will also be found an entertaining description of the ceremonies of the Indians in America, at the time of its first colonisation by the Europeans.

FLAGELLATION, History of, among different Nations, a Narrative of the Strange Customs and Cruelties of the Romans, Greeks, Egyptians, etc., with an Account of its Practice among the Early Christians as a Religious Stimulant and Corrector of Morals, also Anccdotes of Remarkable Cases of Flogging and of celebrated Flagellants. Cr. 8vo, parchment, 6s.

A curious history of whipping inflicted by force, and voluntarily practised by the Monks, Heathens, etc., with Anecdotes of its use by Kings, Bishops, Abbots, etc.

BETTERTON (Thomas, *of the Duke's and United Companies, at the Theatres at Portugal Street, Dorset Gardens, Drury Lane, etc.*) THE LIFE AND TIMES OF, during the latter half of the Seventeenth Century, with such Notices of the Stage and English History, before and after the Restoration, as serve generally to illustrate the subject, by the Editor of the Life of Quin. Cr. 8vo, *portrait by Kneller*, parchment. 3s 6d. 1888

No Life, properly so called, of the great Actor, Thomas Betterton, has before been printed. The book published in 1710 by Giddon, called a " Life of Betterton," is admitted by all to have been only a " Rhapsody " and Rambling Reflections, with supposed conversations. The present volume is a careful effort to supply this deficiency, after long and laborious search.

CLIVE (Mrs. Catherine) The Life of, with an Account of her Adventures on and off the Stage, a Round of her Characters, together with her Correspondence, by PERCY FITZGERALD, M.A., F.S.A., cr. 8vo, *beautiful portrait after Faber, engraved by Alais,* parchment. 3s. 6d.

THEATRICAL.—LIVES of CELEBRATED ACTORS AND ACTRESSES, *portraits,* 8 vols, crown 8vo, vellum. 28s the set, or 3s 6d each

The set embraces the Life of James Quin, with a short history of the stage, his humourous anecdotes, etc.—The Life of Mrs. Abingdon (Miss Barton) celebrated comic actress, with interesting notes on the Irish stage, etc.— The Life and Times of Thomas Betterton, with views of the stage, etc.—An Account of the Life of the Celebrated Actress, Susanah Maria Cibber, with interesting and amusing anecdotes and two remarkable trials—The Life of Miss Annie Cately, the celebrated singing performer of the last century, with her various adventures, amorous intrigues, etc.—The Memoirs and Life, Public and Private of Madame Vestris, with anecdotes, scenes before and behind the curtain, amorous confessions, etc., etc.— The Public and Private Life of Mrs. Jordan, Mistress of the Duke of Clarence (William IV.) with amusing anecdotes, etc.—The Life of Mrs. Catherine Clive, by Percy Fitzgerald, with account of her adventures on and off the stage.

A few LARGE PAPER *copies, double the size of the small paper,* 4to, *india proof portraits,* parchment. £4 4s the set

Only a very few copies were printed of this very desirable size for illustrating. To the collector they are exceedingly welcome, as so many of the fine and rare dramatic portraits used for illustrating are too large to insert in the ordinary 8vo books.

www.ingramcontent.com/pod-product-compliance
Lightning Source LLC
Chambersburg PA
CBHW030544270326
41927CB00008B/1496